ESTATE PUBLICATIONS

DORS

TOWN CENTRE MAPS

Street maps with index
Administrative Districts
Road Map with index
Postcodes

Scale of street plans: 4 Inches to 1 Mile (unless otherwise stated)

Motorway	Every effort has been made to verify the accuracy of information in this book but the publishers cannot accept responsibility for expense or loss caused by an error or omission. Information that will be of assistance to the user of the maps will be welcomed.	Stream / River
'A' Road / Dual		Canal
'B' Road / Dual		One-way Street
Minor Road / Dual		P Car Park
Track		C Public Convenience
Pedestrianized		i Tourist Information
Railway / Station	The representation on these maps of a road, track or path is no evidence of the existence of a right of way.	+ Place of Worship
Footpath		● Post Office

reet plans prepared and published by ESTATE PUBLICATIONS, Bridewell House, TENTERDEN, KENT.
The Publishers acknowledge the co-operation of the local authorities
of towns represented in this atlas.

Ordnance Survey® This product includes mapping data licensed from Ordnance Survey®
with the permission of the Controller of Her Majesty's Stationery Office.

OTHER ATLASES IN THIS COUNTY

COUNTY RED BOOKS contain street maps for each town centre. The street atlases listed below are SUPER & LOCAL RED BOOKS, with comprehensive local coverage.

BOURNEMOUTH

including: Bransgore, Christchurch, Corfe mullen, Ferndown, Milford-on-Sea, New Milton, Poole, Ringwood, Sway, Verwood, Wimborne Minster etc.

NEW FOREST

including: Beaulieu, Brockenhurst, Hythe, Lymington, Lyndhurst, Totton etc.

WEYMOUTH & DORCHESTER

including: Charminster, Chickerell, Easton, Fortuneswell, Preston, Puddletown, Upwey etc.

For a complete title listing please visit our website
www.estate-publications.co.uk

CONTENTS

Scale of street plans: 4 Inches to 1 Mile (unless otherwise stated)

COUNTY RED BOOKS

This atlas is intended for those requiring street maps of the historical and commercial centres of towns within the county. Each locality is normally presented on one or two pages and although, with many small towns, this space is sufficient to portray the whole urban area, the maps of large towns and cities are for centres only and are not intended to be comprehensive. Such coverage is offered in the Super and Local Red Book (see Page 2).

4 DORSET ADMINISTRATIVE DISTRICTS

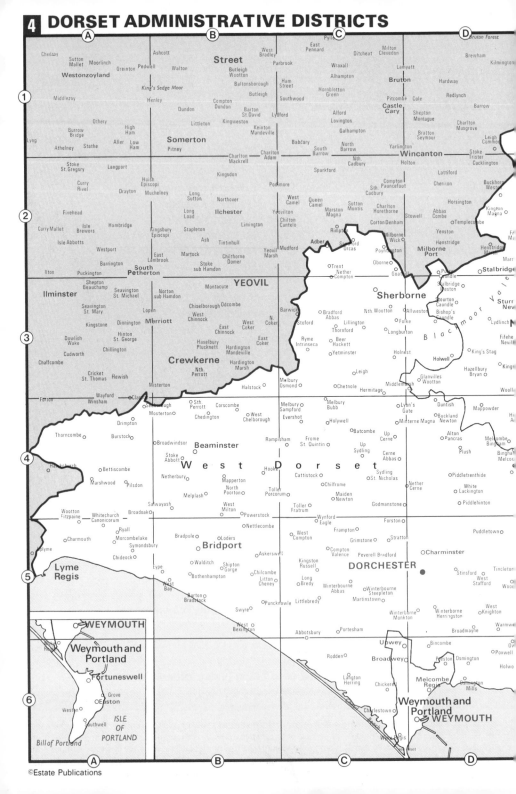

©Estate Publications

GAZETTEER INDEX TO ROAD MAP
with Populations

County of Dorset population 645,166

Place	Grid
Maiden Newton **937**	11 E3
Mannington	13 E2
Manston **160**	8 D3
Manswood	12 D1
Mapperton **20**	10 D3
Mappowder **190**	11 G2
Margaret Marsh **53**	8 D3
Marnhull **1,844**	8 C3
Marshwood **276**	10 B3
Martinstown	11 F4
Melbury Abbas **299**	9 E3
Melbury Bubb **66**	11 E2
Melbury Osmond **168**	11 E2
Melbury Sampford **48**	11 E2
Melcombe Bingham	12 A2
Melcombe Horsey **132**	*
Melcombe Regis **4,413**	11 G6
Melplash	10 D3
Merley	13 E3
Middlemarsh	11 F2
Milborne St Andrew **928**	12 B3
Milton Abbas **542**	12 B2
Milton on Stour	8 D1
Minterne Magna **191**	11 F2
Monkton Up Wimborne	9 G4
More Crichel **167**	12 D1
Moordown **7,473**	13 F3
Morcombelake	10 B4
Moreton **275**	12 A4
Mosterton **526**	10 C2
Motcombe **928**	8 D2
Mudeford **5,693**	13 G4
Nether Cerne **20**	11 F3
Nether Compton **309**	8 A3
Netherbury **1,085**	10 C3
Nettlecombe	10 D4
Newtown **10,742**	13 E4
Norden	12 D5
North Chideock	10 C4
North Wootton **48**	8 A3
Nottington	11 F6
Oborne **116**	8 B3
Okeford Fitzpaine **646**	8 D4
Osmington **517**	11 G5
Osmington Mills	11 G6
Over Compton **157**	*
Owermoigne **434**	12 A5
Pamphill **616**	*
Parkstone **9,039**	13 E4
Parley Cross	13 F3
Pentridge **190**	9 G3
Piddlehinton **468**	11 G3
Piddletrenthide **646**	11 G3
Pilsdon **51**	10 C3
Pimperne **933**	9 E4
Plush	11 G2
Poole **91,921**	12 D4
Poorton **22**	10 D3
Portesham **667**	11 E5
Portland **12,742**	10 B5
Poundbury	11 F4
Powerstock **371**	10 D3
Poxwell **43**	12 A5
Poyntington **145**	8 A3
Preston **4,966**	11 G5
Puddletown **1,130**	11 H4
Pulham **168**	11 G2
Puncknowle **451**	10 D5
Purse Caundle **113**	8 B3
Rampisham **140**	11 E2
Ridge	12 C5
Rodden	11 E5
Ryall	10 C4
Ryme Intrinseca **140**	11 E1
St Ives (with St Leonard's) **6,534**	13 F2
Salwayash	10 C3
Sandbanks	13 E4
Sandford	12 C4
Sandford Orcas **206**	8 A3
Seaborough **56**	10 C2
Seatown	10 C4
Shaftesbury **6,203**	9 E2
Shapwick **195**	12 D2
Sherborne **7,606**	8 A3
Shillingstone **944**	8 D4
Shipton Gorge **344**	10 D4
Silton **139**	8 C1
Sixpenny Handley **1,039**	9 F3
Slepe	12 C4
South Perrott **244**	10 D2
Southbourne **8,310**	13 F4
Southlands	11 F6
Southwell	10 B6
Spetisbury **543**	12 C2
Stalbridge **2,344**	8 C3
Stalbridge Weston	8 C3
Stanbridge	12 D2
Stanton St Gabriel **97**	*
Stapehill **1,843**	13 E2
Steeple **94**	12 C5
Stinsford **324**	11 G4
Stoborough	12 C5
Stoborough Green	12 C5
Stockwood **27**	*
Stoke Abbott **215**	10 C3
Stoke Wake **54**	*
Stokeford	12 B4
Stour Provost **529**	8 D3
Stour Row	8 D3
Stourpaine **598**	9 E4
Stourton Caundle **377**	8 B3
Stratton **316**	11 F4
Stubhampton	9 E4
Studland **471**	13 E5
Sturminster Marshall **1,492**	12 D3
Sturminster Newton **2,579**	8 C4
Sutton Waldron **190**	9 E3
Swanage **9,037**	13 E6
Swyre **110**	10 D5
Sydling St Nicholas **392**	11 F3
Symondsbury **1,092**	10 C4
Tadden	12 D2
Tarrant Crawford **24**	12 C2
Tarrant Gunville **248**	9 E4
Tarrant Hinton **185**	9 F4
Tarrant Keyneston **290**	12 C2
Tarrant Launceston **608**	9 F4
Tarrant Monkton **1,293**	12 D1
Tarrant Rawston **55**	12 C1
Tarrant Rushton **108**	12 C2
Thorncombe **624**	10 B2
Thornicombe	12 B2
Thornford **804**	8 A4
Three Legged Cross	13 E1
Tincleton **139**	12 A4
Todber **86**	8 D3
Toller Fratrum **27**	11 E3
Toller Porcorum **345**	11 E3
Toller Whelme	10 D3
Tolpuddle **317**	12 A3
Trent **304**	8 A3
Trickett's Cross **5,338**	13 F2
Turners Puddle **57**	12 B3
Turnworth **65**	12 B1
Tyneham	12 C6
Up Cerne **11**	11 F2
Up Sydling	11 F3
Uploders	10 D4
Upton & Lytchett Minster **7,327**	12 D4
Upwey	11 F5
Verwood **10,446**	9 H4
Walditch	10 D4
Wareham **5,644**	12 C4
Wareham St Martin **2,544**	*
Warmwell **98**	12 A5
Waterloo	12 D3
Waytown	10 C3
West Bay	10 C4
West Bexington	10 D5
West Chelborough **33**	10 D2
West Compton **37**	11 E4
West Holme	12 C5
West Knighton **408**	11 G5
West Lulworth **838**	12 B5
West Milton	10 D3
West Moors **6,878**	13 E2
West Morden **345**	12 C3
West Orchard **77**	8 D3
West Parley **3,510**	13 E3
West Stafford **244**	11 G4
West Stour **159**	8 C2
Westbourne **6,832**	13 E4
Weston	10 B6
Weymouth **44,098**	11 G6
Whatcombe	12 B2
Whitcombe **64**	*
White Lackington	11 G3
Whitechurch Canonicorum **669**	10 B2
Wigbeth	13 E1
Wimborne Minster **6,292**	12 D2
Wimborne St Giles **368**	9 G4
Winfrith Newburgh **705**	12 B5
Winterborne Carne **47**	*
Winterborne Clenston **45**	12 B2
Winterborne Herrinsgton **26**	11 G5
Winterborne Houghton **198**	12 B2
Winterborne Kingston **491**	12 B3
Winterborne Monkton **63**	11 F5
Winterborne St Martin **769**	*
Winterborne Stickland **542**	12 B2
Winterborne Whitechurch **594**	12 B2
Winterborne Zelston **133**	12 C3
Winterbourne Abbas **295**	11 F4
Winterbourne Steepleton **282**	11 F4
Winton **7,795**	13 F3
Witchampton **399**	12 D1
Wonston	11 G2
Woodlands **537**	13 E1
Woodsford **89**	12 A4
Woodyates	9 G3
Wool **4,435**	12 B5
Woolland **79**	12 A1
Wootton Fitzpaine **295**	10 B3
Worth Matravers **603**	12 D6
Wraxall **41**	*
Wyke **2,045**	8 D2
Wyke Regis **5,168**	10 B5
Wynford Eagle **57**	11 E3
Yetminster **1,017**	8 A4

Population figures are based upon the 1991 census and relate to the local authority area or parish as constituted at that date Boundaries of the districts are shown on pages 4-5. Places with no population figure form part of a larger local authority area or parish.

Population figures in bold type.

*Place not included on map pages 8-13 due to limitation of space

7

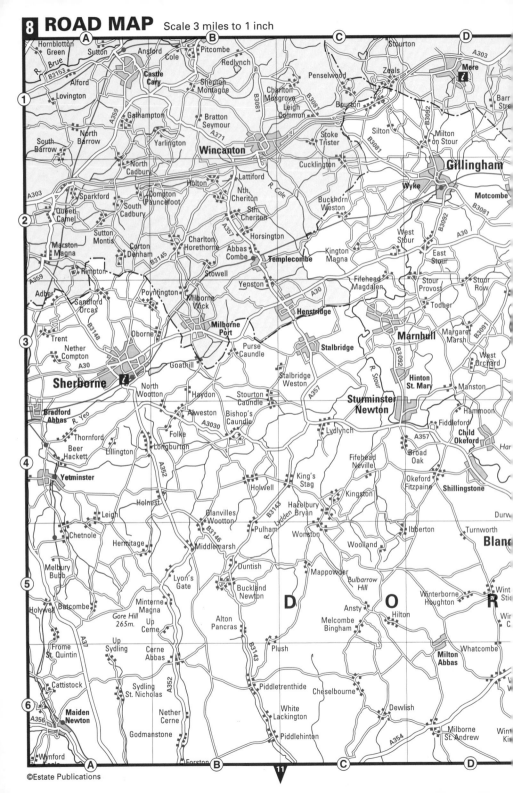

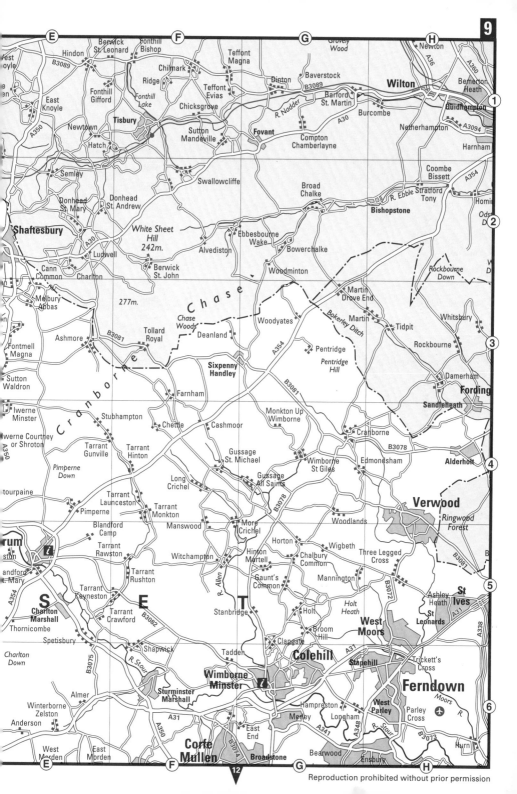

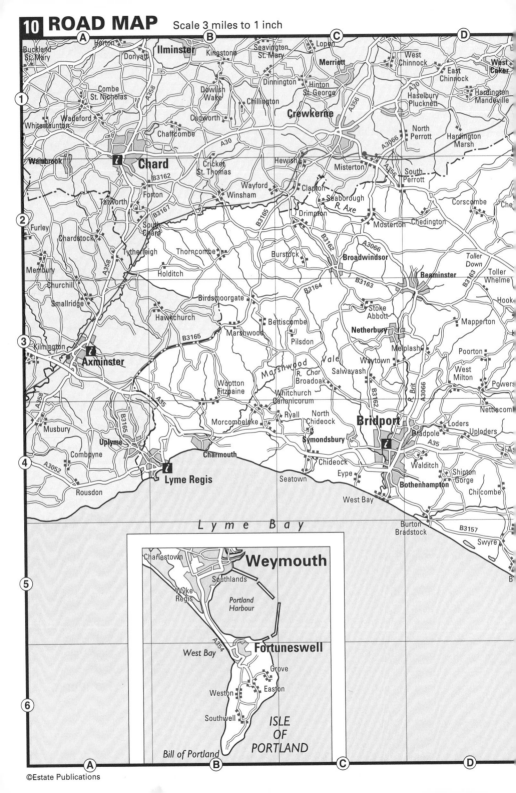

Buckland St. Mary
Horton
Donyatt
Ilminster
Kingstone
Seavington St. Mary
Lopen
West Chinnock
East Chinnock
West Coker
Combe St. Nicholas
Dowlish Wake
Dinnington
Hinton St. George
Merriott
Haselbury Plucknett
Hardington Mandeville
Wadeford
Chillington
Crewkerne
Whitestaunton
Cudworth
Chaffcombe
North Perrott
Hardington Marsh
Wambrook
Chard
Cricket St. Thomas
Hewish
Misterton
South Perrott
B3162
Wayford
Clapton
Corscombe
Che
Forton
Winsham
Seaborough
R. Axe
Tatworth
B3167
Chedington
Furley
South Chard
Drimpton
Mosterton
Chardstock
Burstock
B3162
A3066
Broadwindsor
Toller Down
Tytherleigh
Thorncombe
B3165
Beaminster
B3163
Toller Whelme
Membury
Holditch
B3163
Churchill
Birdsmoorgate
B3164
Stoke Abbott
Hook
Smallridge
Hawkchurch
Bettiscombe
Mapperton
Kilmington
B3165
Marshwood
Pilsdon
Netherbury
Poorton
Axminster
Wootton Fitzpaine
Marshwood Vale
R. Char
Broadoak
Waytown
Salwayash
Melplash
West Milton
Powers
A35
Whitchurch Canonicorum
R. Brit
A3066
Nettlecom
Musbury
B3165
Morcombelake
Ryall
North Chideock
Bridport
Loders
Uploders
A356
Uplyme
Symondsbury
Bradpole
A35
Combpyne
A3052
Charmouth
Chideock
Eype
Waditch
Shipton Gorge
Chilcombe
Rousdon
Lyme Regis
Seatown
West Bay
Bothenhampton
Burton Bradstock
Swyre
B3157

Lyme Bay

Charlestown
Weymouth
Southlands
Wyke Regis
Portland Harbour
West Bay
Fortuneswell
A354
Grove
Weston
Easton
Southwell
ISLE OF PORTLAND
Bill of Portland

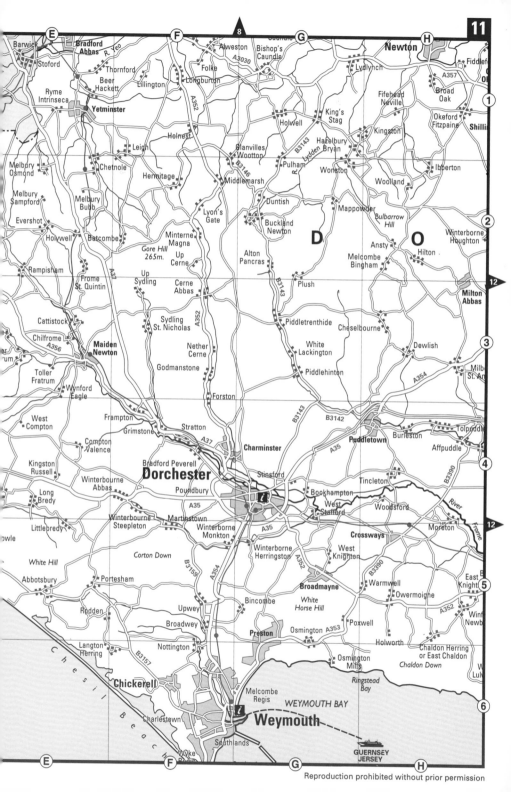

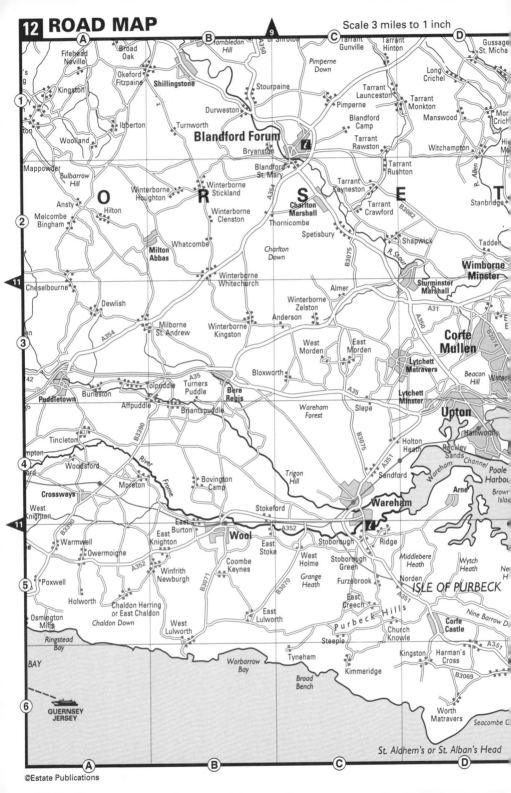

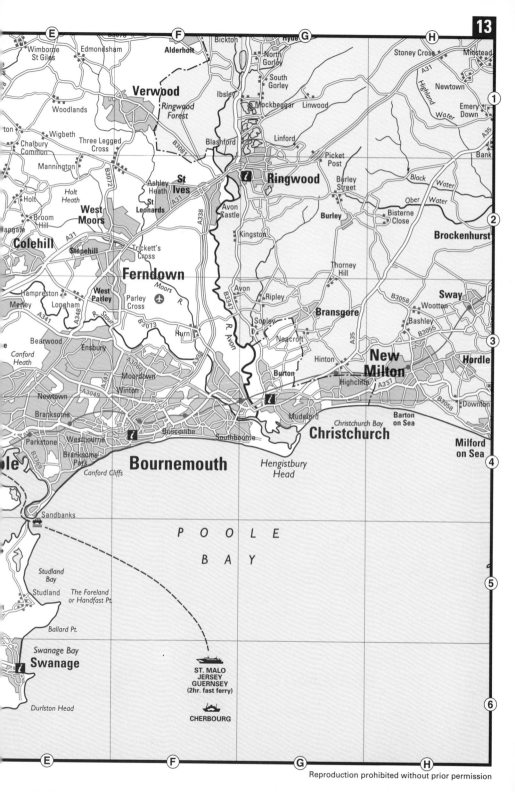

E F G H

Wimborne St Giles
Edmondsham
Alderholt
Bickton
Hyde
Stoney Cross
Minstead

North Gorley
A31
Newtown

Verwood
Ibsley
South Gorley
Highland
Emery Down

Woodlands
Ringwood Forest
Mockbeggar
Linwood
Water

Wigbeth
Blashford
Linford
A35

Chalbury Common
Three Legged Cross
B3081
Picket Post
Bank

Mannington
Ashley Heath
St Ives
Ringwood
Burley Street
Black Water

Holt
Holt Heath
St Leonards
Avon Castle
Burley
Ober Water
Bisterne Close

West Moors
Kingston
Brockenhurst

Broom Hill
Colehill
Stapehill
Trickett's Cross

Hampreston
West Parley
Moors R.
Thorney Hill
Sway

Merley
Longham
Parley Cross
Avon
Ripley
B3058
Wootten

Bearwood
Ensbury
Hurn
Sopley
Bransgore
Bashley
B3055

Canford Heath
Moordown
R. Avon
Neacroft
New Milton
Hordle

Newtown
Winton
Hinton
Highcliffe
A337
Downton

Branksome
Burton
Mudeford

Parkstone
Westbourne
Boscombe
Southbourne
Christchurch
Milford on Sea

Branksome Park
Bournemouth
Christchurch Bay
Barton on Sea

Canford Cliffs
Hengistbury Head

Sandbanks

P O O L E
B A Y

Studland Bay
Studland
The Foreland or Handfast Pt.

Ballard Pt.

Swanage Bay
Swanage

Durlston Head

ST. MALO
JERSEY
GUERNSEY
(2hr. fast ferry)

CHERBOURG

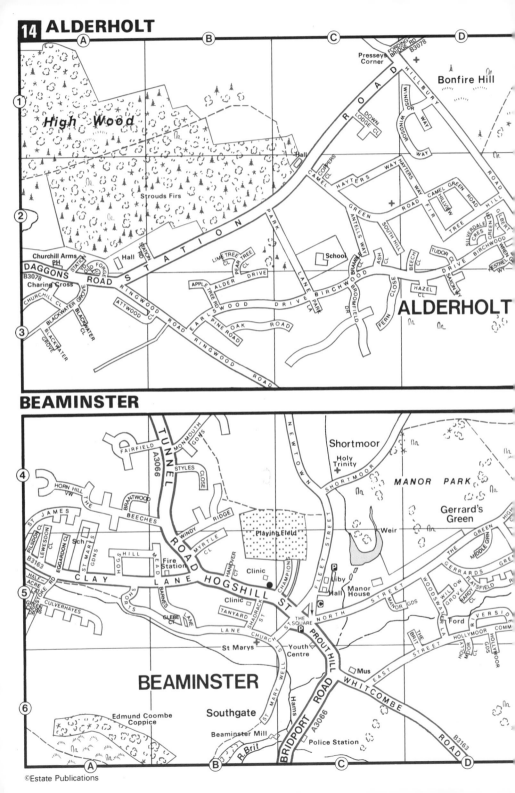

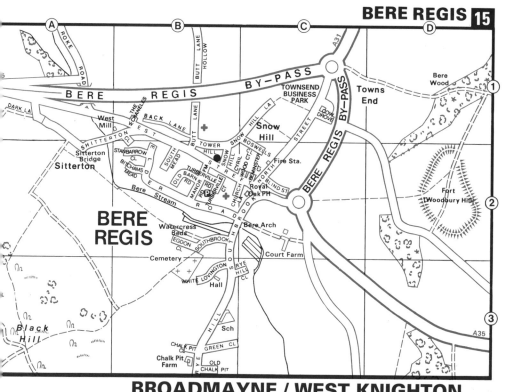

BROADMAYNE / WEST KNIGHTON

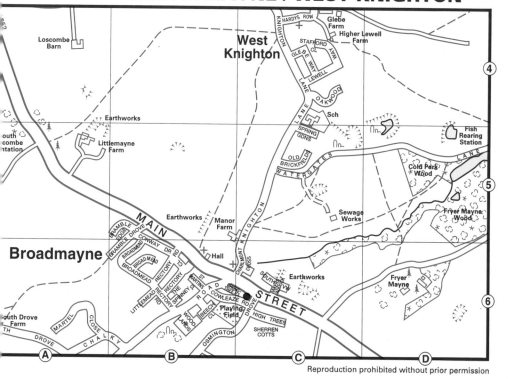

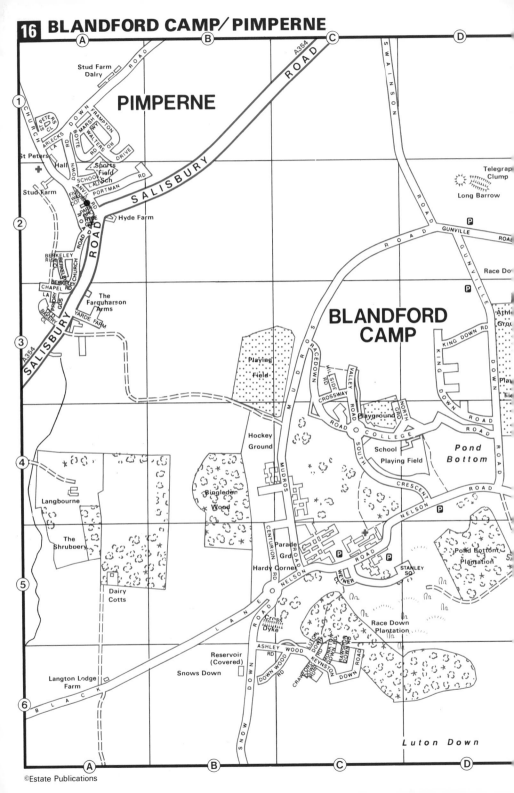

PIMPERNE

BLANDFORD CAMP

Stud Farm Dairy

St Peters
Hall
Stud Farm
Hyde Farm

The Farquharson Arms

Berkeley Rise
Chapel Rd

Playing Field

Hockey Ground

Langbourne
The Shrubbery

Bingleden Wood

Dairy Cotts

Langton Lodge Farm

Reservoir (Covered)
Snows Down

Cross Dyke

Parade Grd
Hardy Corner

Playground
School
Playing Field

Pond Bottom

Pond Bottom Plantation

Race Down Plantation

Stanley Sq

Telegraph Clump
Long Barrow

Gunville Road
Race Down

King Down Rd
Athletic Ground

SALISBURY ROAD
A354

SWAINSON ROAD

MUDROS ROAD

NELSON ROAD

CENTURION RD

CRESCENT ROAD

COLLEGE ROAD

KING DOWN ROAD

Luton Down

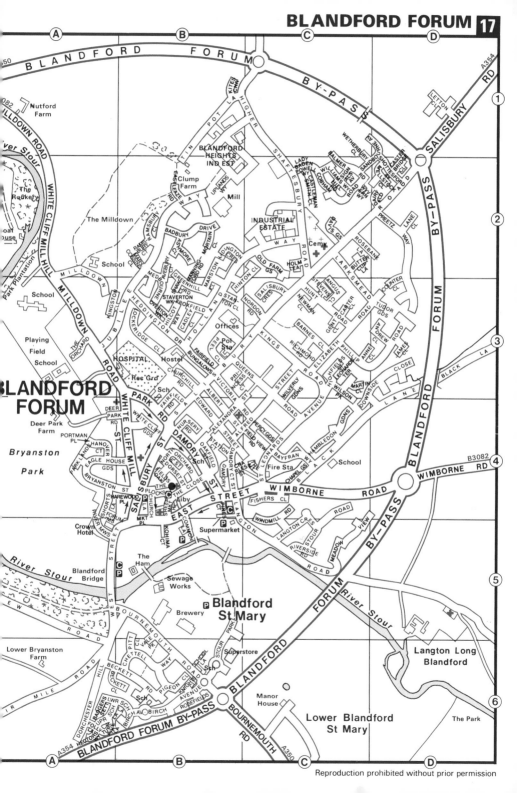

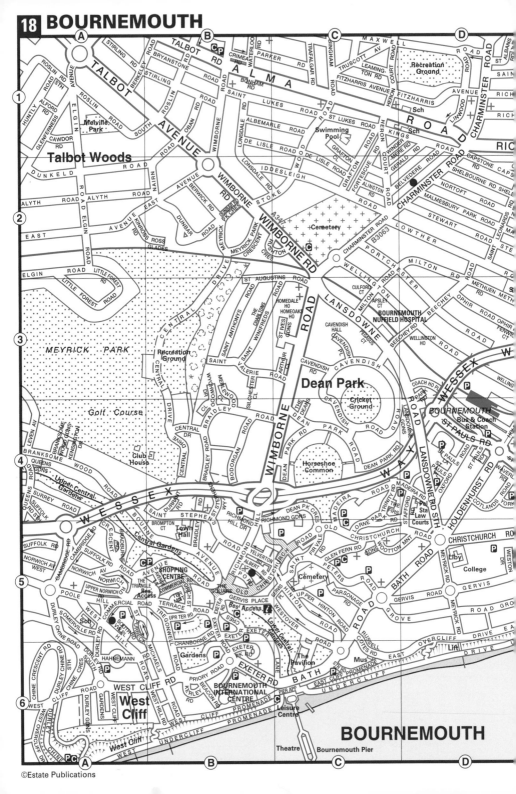

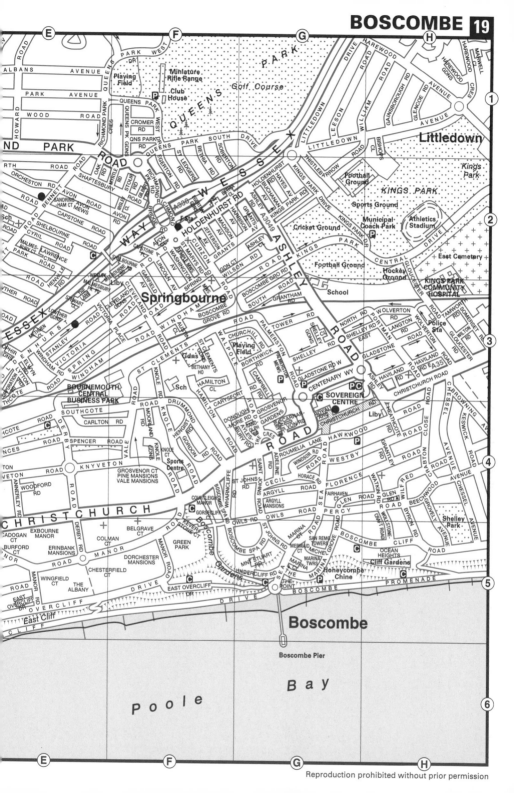

BOSCOMBE 19

Boscombe

Boscombe Pier

Poole Bay

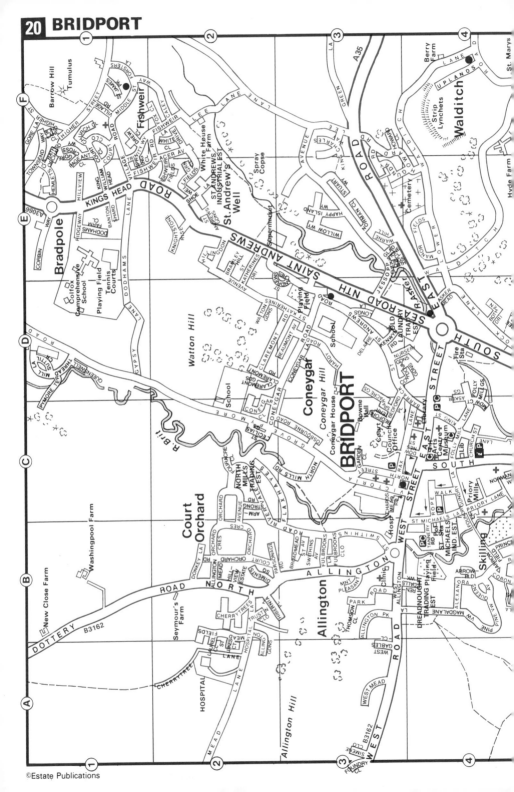

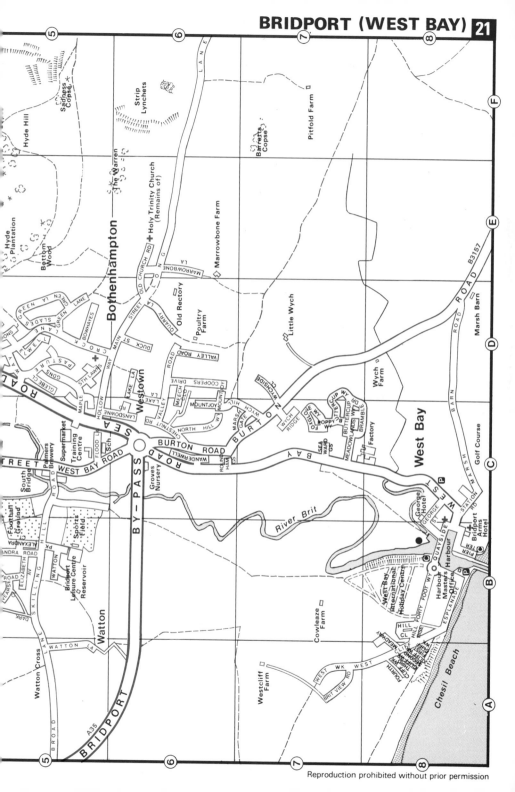

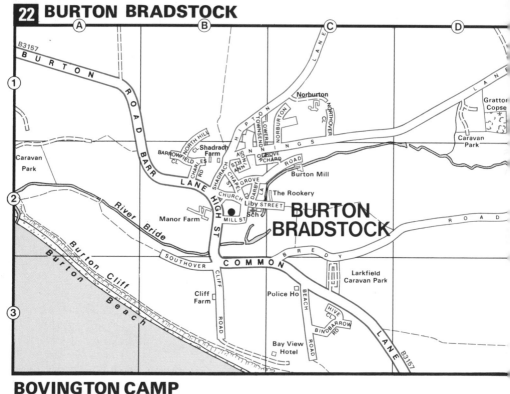

BOVINGTON CAMP

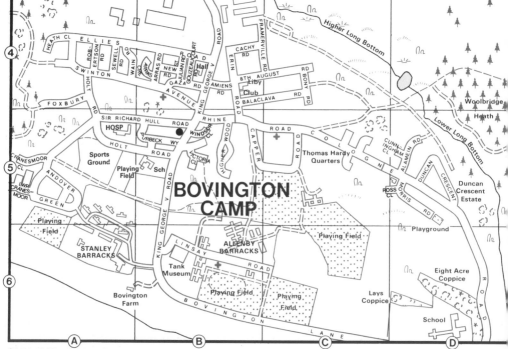

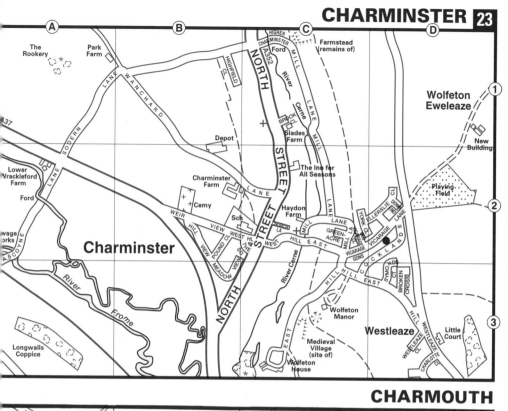

CHARMOUTH

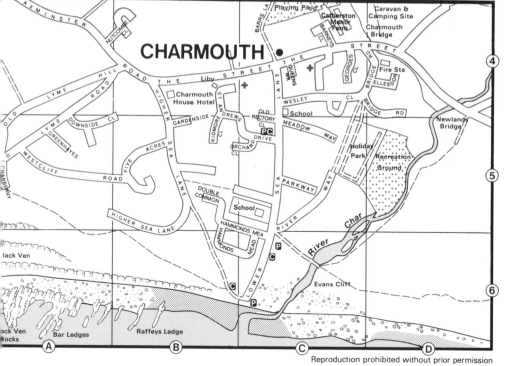

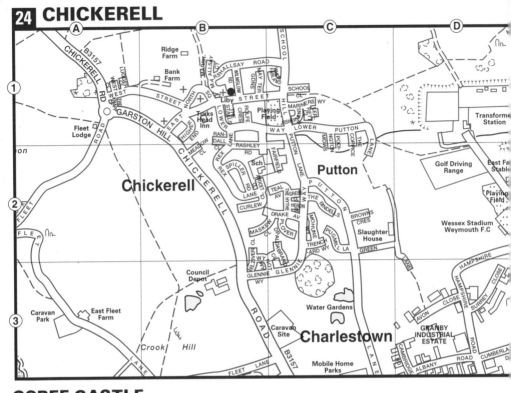

CHICKERELL RD
B3157
LODGE WEST STREET
GARSTON HILL
Fleet Lodge
Ridge Farm
Bank Farm
MARSHALLSAY ROAD
NORTH SQ
WILMSLOW
MAY TERR
SCHOOL LANE
SCHOOL STREET
Liby
Turks Head Inn
EAST STREET
MEADOW CL
HIGHER END
TOWER STREET
RANDALL
REX LANE
REX LANE
RASHLEY RD
Sch
SPILLER RD
FAIRFIELD
CURLEW LANE
TEAL AV
HERON
PLOVER
DRAKE AV
MASKEW CL
GLEBE WY
GLENNIE WY
GLENNIE
GLENNIE WY
Council Depot

Chickerell

Caravan Park
East Fleet Farm
Crook Hill
FLEET
FLEM

2
3

LIBY STREET
RIFLE CRES
FISHERMENS
PLAYING FIELD
MARINERS WY
LOWER MDWS
PUTTON LANE
THE COPPICE
POOL NOOK
PUTTON LANE
LOWER WAY
FAIRFIELD
THE GREEN
PUTTON LA
THE BINDELS
MICHANE
TRENCH YARD WY
PUGMILL LA
BROWNS CRES
Slaughter House
GREEN
LANE
Water Gardens
Caravan Site

Putton

Charlestown

B3157
FLEET LANE
Mobile Home Parks
LANE

Transformer Station
Golf Driving Range
East Fa Stabl
Playing Field
Wessex Stadium Weymouth F.C
HAMPSHIRE CLOSE
HAMPSHIRE CLOSE
SURREY
CLOSE
AVON
CAMBRIDGE
ALBANY ROAD
GRANBY INDUSTRIAL ESTATE
ROAD
CUMBERLA

CORFE CASTLE

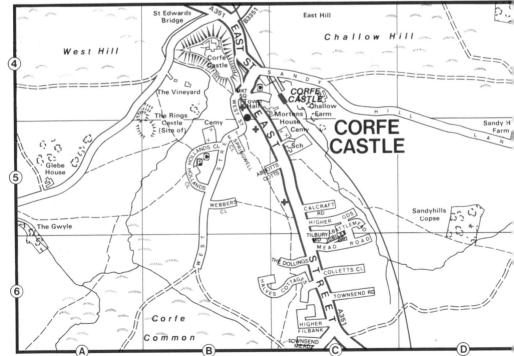

A351
St Edwards Bridge
EAST ST
B3351
East Hill
Challow Hill
West Hill
Corfe Castle
The Vineyard
The Rings Castle (Site of)
Cemy
HOLLANDS CL
Glebe House
The Gwyle
WEBBERS CL
MKT SQ
Town Hall
WEST ST
SANDY
CORFE CASTLE
Mortans House
Ohallow Farm
Cemy
Sch
HILL
LANE
Sandy H Farm
SPRINGWELL
EAST
ABBOTTS COTTS
CALCRAFT RD
HIGHER GDS
TILBURY RD
BATTLEME
JUBILEE
MEAD ROAD
Sandyhills Copse
THE DOLLINGS
STREET
WEST STREET
COLLETTS CL
HALVES COTTAGE
TOWNSEND RD
A351
HIGHER FILBANK
TOWNSEND MEAD
Corfe Common

CORFE CASTLE

4
5
6

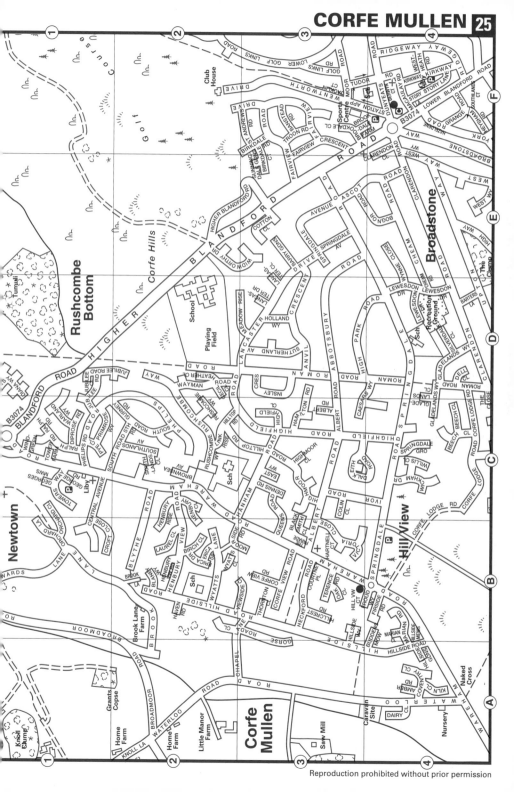

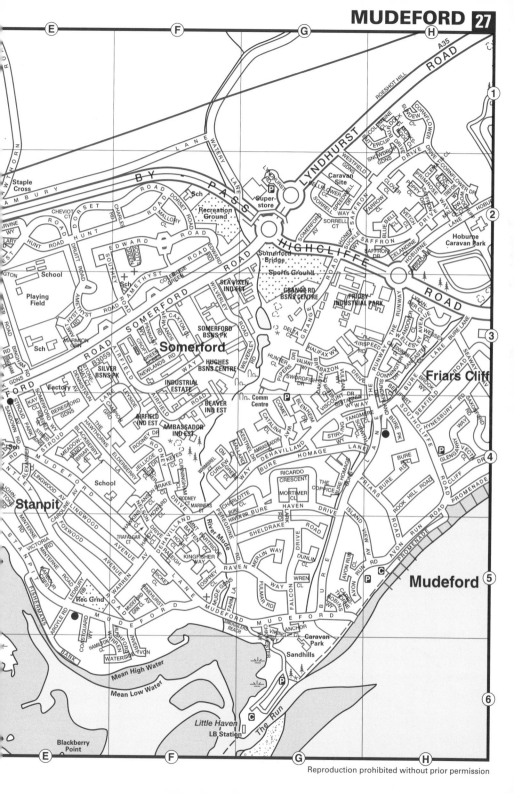

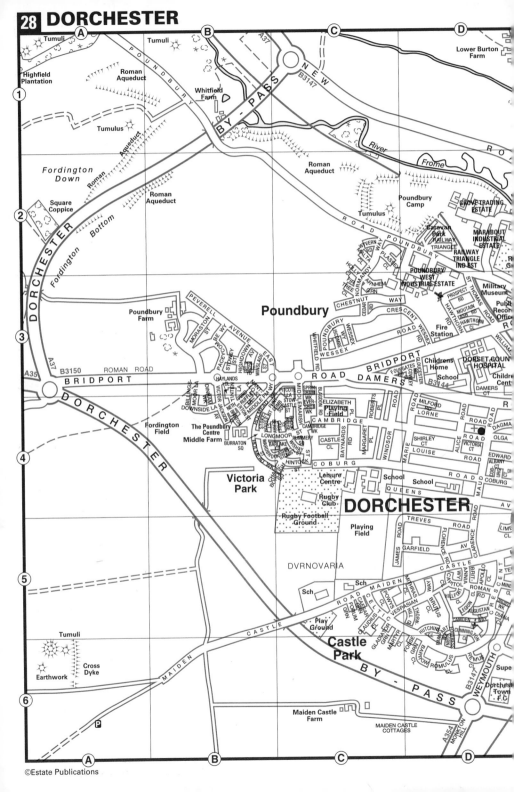

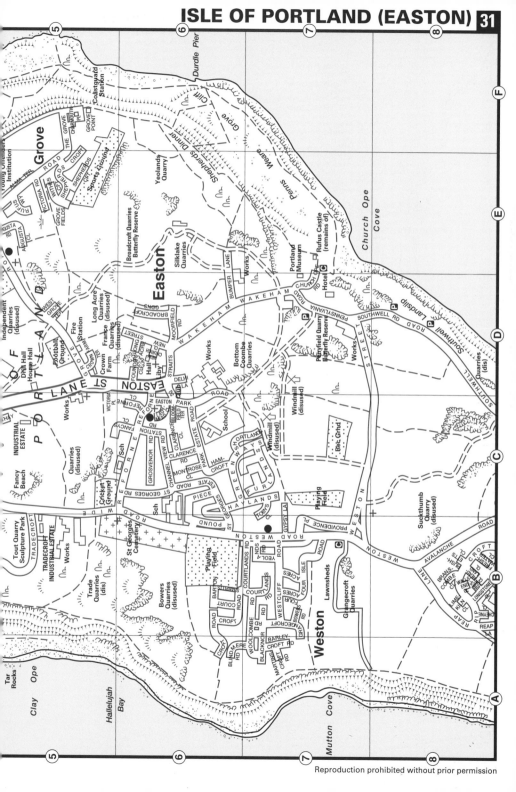

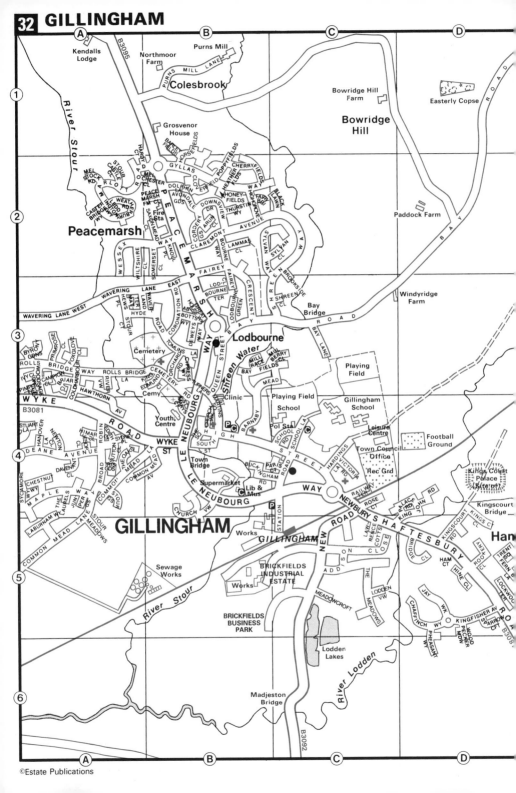

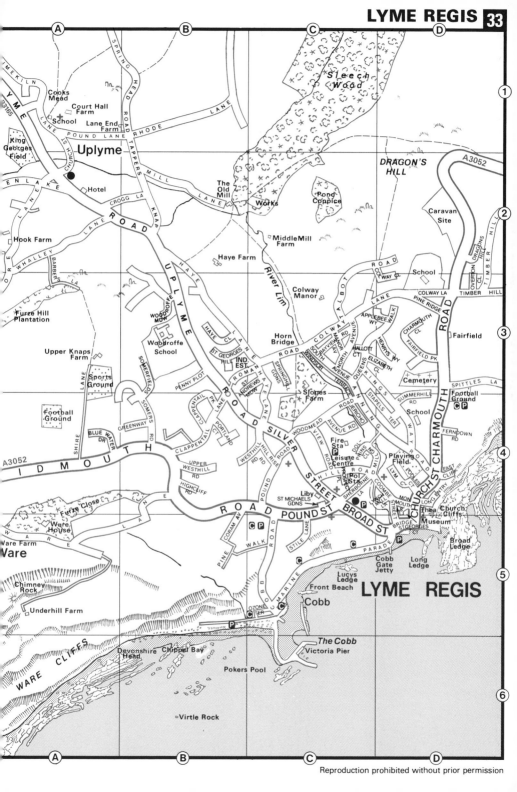

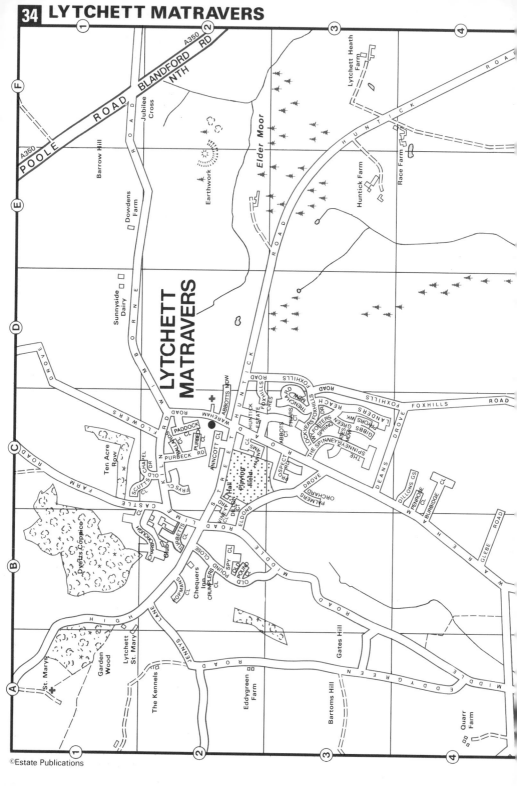

LYTCHETT MATRAVERS

©Estate Publications

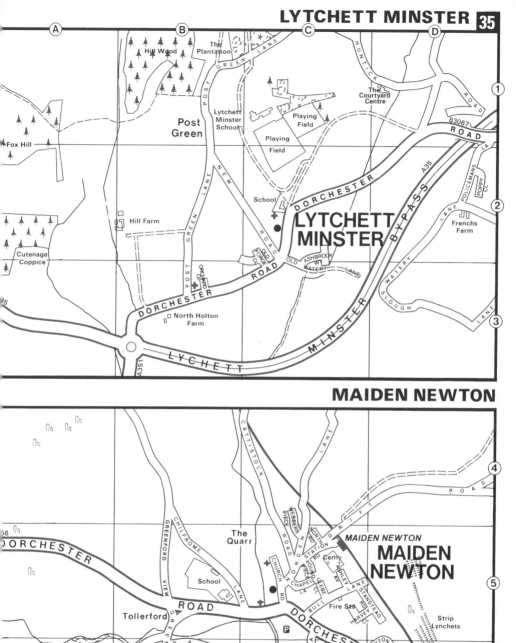

MAIDEN NEWTON

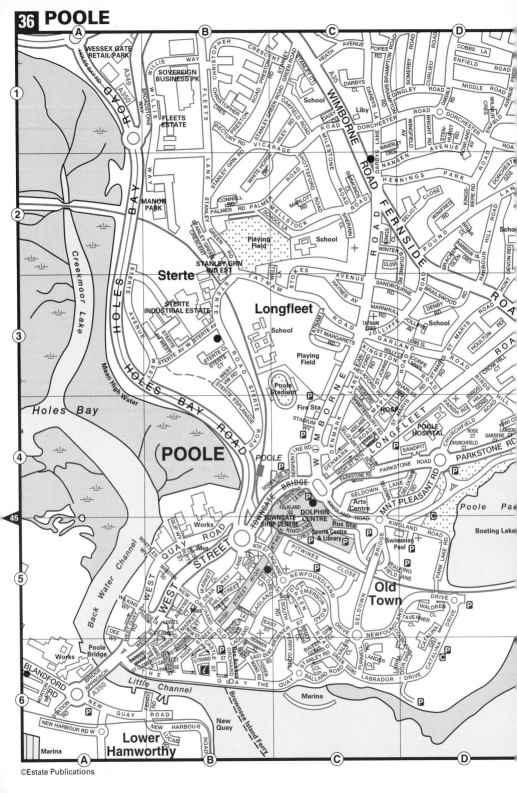

PRESTON 37

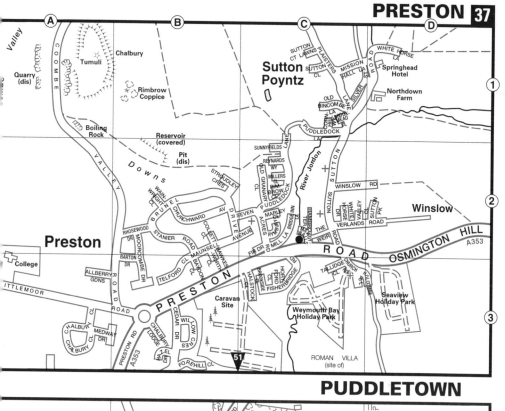

PRESTON

Valley

(A)
(B)
(C)
(D)

COOMBE VALLEY

Tumuli
Chalbury

Quarry (dis)
Rimbrow Coppice

Sutton Poyntz

SUTTON CT LAWNS
PAISTERS
SUTTON CL
MISSION HALL
WHITE HORSE
SILVER RD
Springhead Hotel
Northdown Farm

(1)

Boiling Rock

Reservoir (covered)

OLD BINCOMBE
CORN LA
MEAD
PUDDLEDOCK LA

Pit (dis)

Downs

VALLEY

SUNNYFIELDS
REYNARDS
STROUDLEY CRES
OLD GRANARY CL
MILLERS CL
RIMBROW
WY
River Jordan
SUTTON RD
WINSLOW RD

(2)

WAIN
WRIGHT
BRUNEL
CHURCHWARD AV
COLLET CL
SEVEN ACRES
MARLEY
PUDDLEDOCK
MILL LA
RYN
HAMBRO TERR
INN LA
BRIDGE
SUTTON DR
HORSE DR
WHITE VALLEY
VERLANDS
SUTTON PK
SUTTON ROAD

Winslow

Preston

RHOSEWOOD DR
STANIER
MOORCOMBE DR
HAWKES
WYATT
FIR DR
AVENUE
DRIVE
THE WEIR
ROAD

OSMINGTON HILL
A353

College

BARTON DR
ALLBERRY GDNS
MAUNSEL
TELFORD CL
BARDON CL
PRESTON ROAD
HALSTOCK
BROADSIDE
FERN
HORTON
FISHERBRIDGE
FORD
TALLIDGE CL
CHURCH RD
MILCOMBE

PRESTON ROAD

ITTLEMOOR

Caravan Site

Seaview Holiday Park

(3)

CHALBURY CL
MEDWAY DR
CHALBURY
PRESTON RD A353
CHALBURY LODGE
CEDAR DR
WILLOW CRES
FOREHILL CL

51

Weymouth Bay Holiday Park

ROMAN VILLA (site of)

PUDDLETOWN

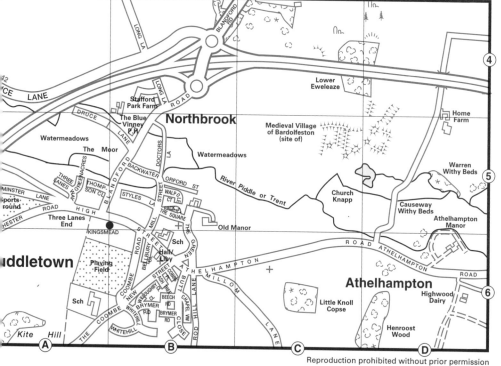

(A)
(B)
(C)
(D)

BLANDFORD

42

CE LANE

LONG LA
ROAD

Lower Eweleaze

Home Farm

(4)

DRUCE
Stafford Park Farm

The Blue Vinney P.H.

Northbrook

Medieval Village of Bardolfeston (site of)

Warren Withy Beds

(5)

Watermeadows

The Moor

BLANDFORD BACKWATER
DOCTORS LA
ORFORD ST
WALPO
STREET
STYLES
THE SQUARE

Watermeadows

River Piddle or Trent

Church Knapp

Causeway Withy Beds

Athelhampton Manor

MINSTER LANE
sports round
THREE LANES
THOMP SON CL
HIGH
ROAD
Three Lanes End
KINGSMEAD
BELL BURY
MILL STREET
HESTER

ddletown

Playing Field

Sch
Libry
Hall
Old Manor

ROAD ATHELHAMPTON

THE COOMBE
NEW
WHITEHILL RD
BRYMER
BEECH
BRYMER RD
BUTT LANE
CHAPEL W
ATHELHAMPTON
MILLOM
HILL ROAD
LANE

Athelhampton

Sch

Little Knoll Copse

Highwood Dairy

(6)

Kite Hill

(A)
(B)
(C)
(D)

Henroost Wood

Reproduction prohibited without prior permission

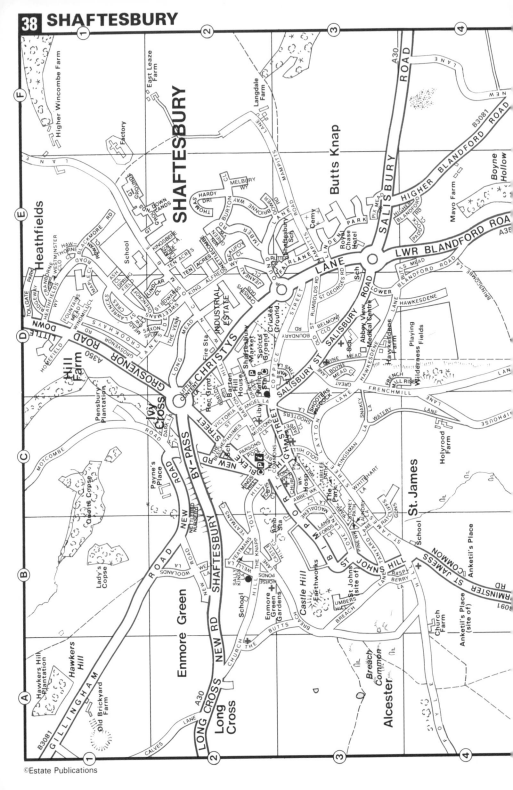

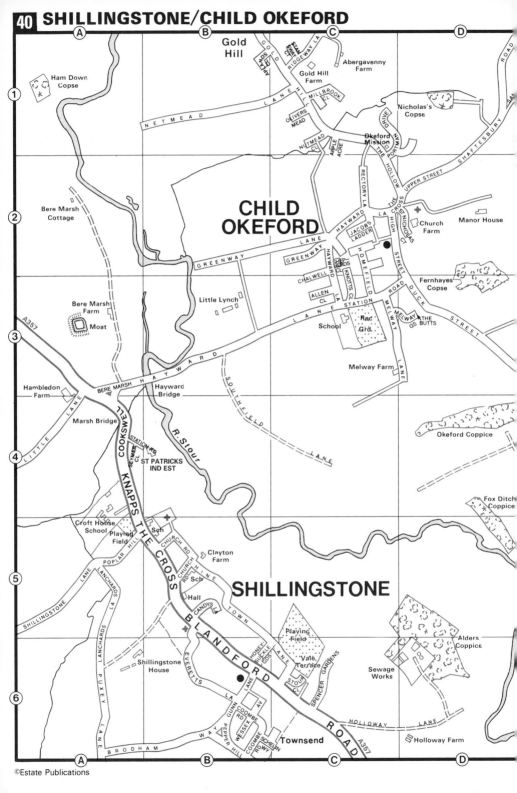

Gold Hill

Ham Down Copse

NETMEAD LANE

GOLD HILL ROAD

GOLD HILL LANE

STAN SWA

RIDGEWAY LA

Abergavenny Farm

Gold Hill Farm

MILLBROOK CL

OLIVERS MEAD

NUTMEAD CL

APPLE ACRE

Okeford Mission

Nicholas's Copse

THE PORTMAN

THE HOLLOW

DRIVE NW

RECTORY LA

UPPER STREET

SHAFTESBURY

Bere Marsh Cottage

CHILD OKEFORD

GREENWAY LANE

GREENWAY

HAYWARD LANE

HAYWARD CL

CHALWELL CL

JACOBS LADDER

SHEPHERDS CL

KNOTS CL

HOMEFIELD

THE CROSS

ST NICHOLAS

Church Farm

Manor House

HIGH STREET

ROAD

DUCK STREET

Fernhayes Copse

Little Lynch

ALLEN CL

STATION LANE

School

Rec Grd

MELWAY

MELWAY

GS BUTTS

THE BUTTS

Bere Marsh Farm

Moat

A357

HAYWARD ROAD

BERE MARSH

SOUTH FIELD LANE

Melway Farm

MELWAY LANE

Hambledon Farm

LITTLE LANE

COOKSWELL LANE

Marsh Bridge

Hayward Bridge

R. Stour

STATION RD

SEYMER CL

ST PATRICKS IND EST

Okeford Coppice

Fox Ditch Coppice

KNAPPS THE CROSS

SHILLINGSTONE LANE

LANCHARDS LA

POPLAR HILL

Croft House School

Playing Field

Sch

CHURCH RD

PINE RD

Sch

Clayton Farm

SHILLINGSTONE

Hall

PUXEY LANE

LANCHARDS LANE

BLANDFORD

CANDYS LA

CHURCH HILL

TOWN LANE

Playing Field

Vale Terrace

SPENCER GARDENS

STOUR CL

Sewage Works

Alders Coppice

Shillingstone House

EVERETTS LA

HONEYSUCKLE CLOSE

COOMBE RD

COOMBE AV

WESSEX AV

PEPPER HILL

GUNN LA

WAY

BRODHAM

COOMBE SCHELIN ROWY

Townsend

HOLLOWAY LANE

ROAD

A357

Holloway Farm

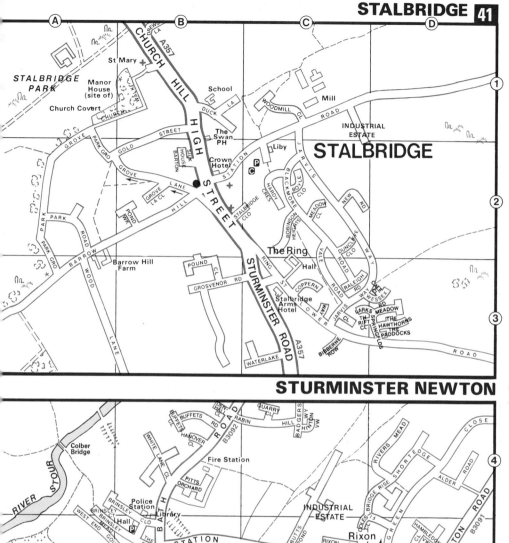

STURMINSTER NEWTON

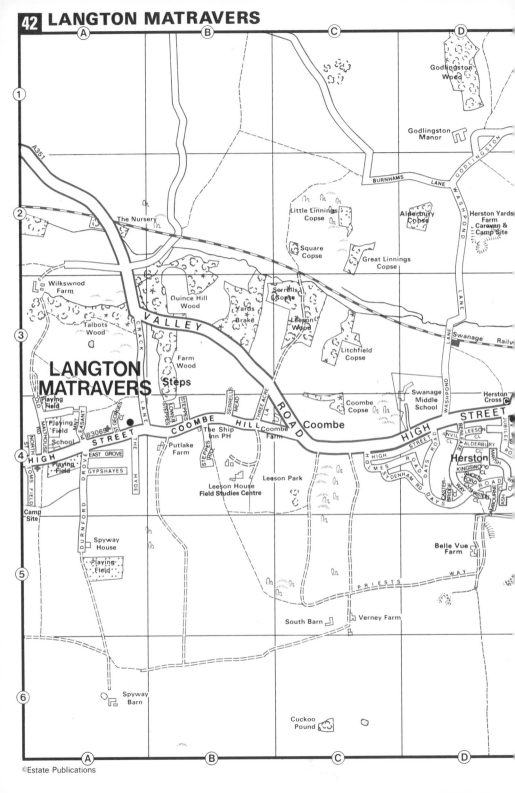

Godlingston Wood

Godlingston Manor

BURNHAMS LANE

The Nursery

Little Linnings Copse

Alderbury Copse

Herston Yards Farm Caravan & Camp Site

Square Copse

Great Linnings Copse

Wilkswood Farm

Quince Hill Wood

Serrells Copse

Yards Brake

Leeson Wood

Talbots Wood

Farm Wood Steps

Litchfield Copse

Swanage Railw

LANGTON MATRAVERS

Playing Field

Playing Field

School

Coombe Copse

Swanage Middle School

Herston Cross

B3069

EAST GROVE

GYPSHAYES

STREET

The Ship Inn PH

Putlake Farm

Coombe Farm

Coombe

STREET

HIGH STREET

Herston

HIGH STREET

Playing Field

Camp Site

Leeson House Field Studies Centre

Leeson Park

Belle Vue Farm

Spyway House

Playing Field

PRIESTS WAY

South Barn

Verney Farm

Spyway Barn

Cuckoo Pound

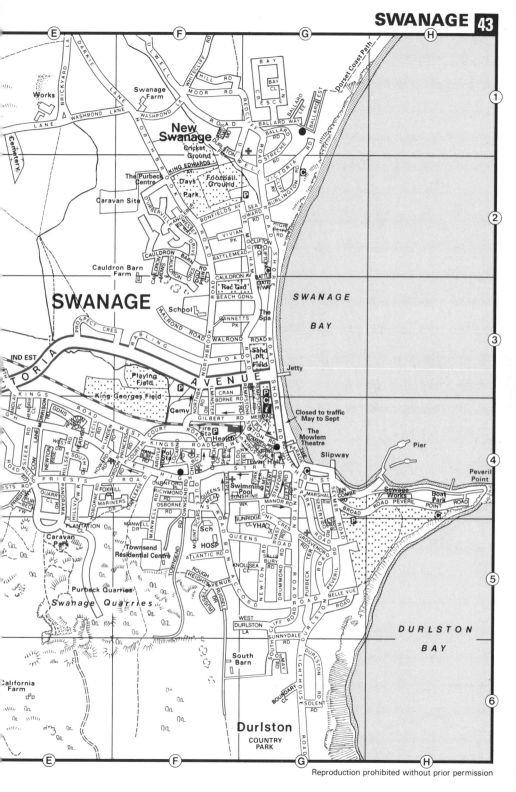

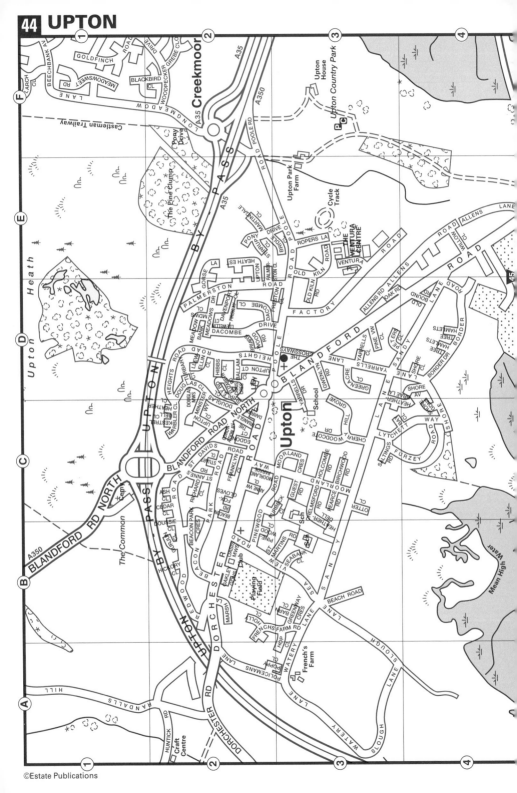

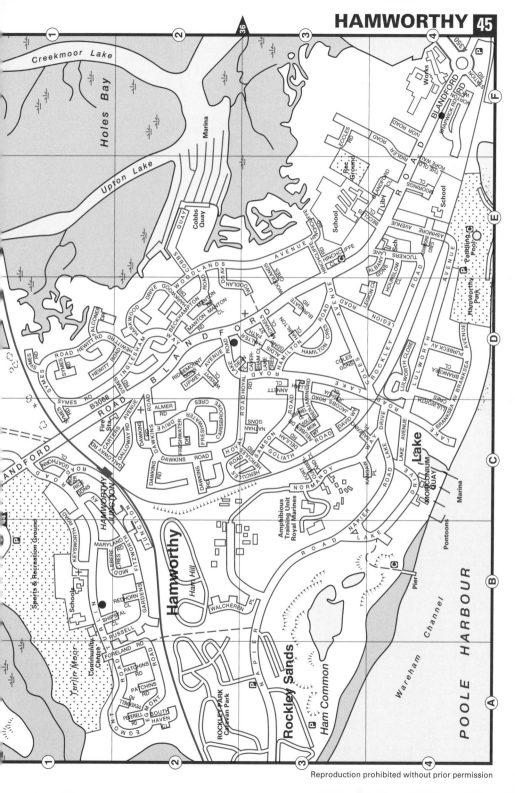

Creekmoor Lake

Holes Bay

Upton Lake

Marina

Cobbs Quay

QUAY

COBBS

WOODLANDS DR

HARKWOOD DRIVE

BECKHAMPTON ROAD

MANTON RD

MANTON CL

WOODLANDS RD

WOODLANDS CRES

AVENUE

HINCHLIFFE

HINCHLIFFE RD

HINCHLIFFE CL

BLANDFORD ROAD

Works

BLANDFORD

NORTON RD

A350

P

STATION RD

Rapwick RD

IVOR ROAD

BLANDFORD ROAD

RIGLEY ROAD

ROAD

THE OLD ROPE WALK

MOORINGS

CT

School

ECCLES RD

Rec. Ground

Libry

ECCLES RD

BECCLES RD

School

ASHMORE AVENUE

ALBANY RD

TUCKERS LANE

HOUNSLOW CL

Sch

HAMWORTHY Park

Paddling Pool

P

AVENUE

PURBECK AV

BRANKSEA AV

BRANKSEA AV

LULWORTH CRES

BLANDFORD ROAD

ROCKLEY ROAD

LEGION CL

LEGION RD

LEGION ROAD

STOKES AVENUE

LULWORTH CLOSE

LULWORTH AVENUE

HAMILTON CRES

HAMILTON RD

BURGATE RD

COLES GDNS

DELILAH RD

ALOISI GDNS

BEAM CL

LAKE

SIOLA

WINSPIT CL

RIDGEMONT GDNS

LUPWEY AVENUE

FALTER PATH

LAKE ROAD

CAYER

HEWITT RD

HEWITT BROAD RD

INGLESHAM AVENUE

BLANDFORD ROAD

FALCONER DR

SYMES RD

SYMES RD

ROAD

SYMES RD

SYMES

B3068

ROAD

Fire Sta.

CARTERS AVENUE

GALLOWAY RD

DAWKINS DRIVE

FRESHWATER DR

FRESHWATER CRES

CARISBROOKE AVE

ALMER RD

DAWKINS RD

DAWKINS ROAD

DAWKINS RD

ROAD

ROYAL

NATHAN GDNS

ANNETT RD

JACOBS ROAD

SCHOOL RD

LAMINGTON RD

HERCULES RD

NELSON RD

SAMSON RD

GOLIATH RD

DAVID RD

KANGAW PL

DUKE RD

ROYAL RD

NORMANDY RD

FORT CUMBERLAND RD

NAPIER ROAD

LAKE ROAD

LAKE AVENUE

LAKE DRIVE

DRIVE

Lake

Marina

Millennium Quay

Pontoons

GALLOWAY RD

RICE RD

EDNS

GOATHORN ROAD

HAWTHORN CL

HAMWORTHY JUNCTION

MARYLAND RD

KEYSWORTH

LEBERE CRES

MIDD

FITZWORTH

GARDENS

JUNCTION

Schools

Sports & Recreation Ground

P

Turlin Moor

Community Centre

REDHORN CL

SHIPSTAL CL

RUSSELL RD

FORELAND RD

PATCHINS RD

PATCHINS RD

PEVERELL RD

EGMONT RD

SOUTH HAVEN CL

ROCKLEY PARK Caravan Park

Hamworthy

Ham Hill

WALCHEREN PL

NAPIER ROAD

Amphibious Training Unit Royal Marines

Rockley Sands

Ham Common

Pier

C

POOLE HARBOUR

Wareham Channel

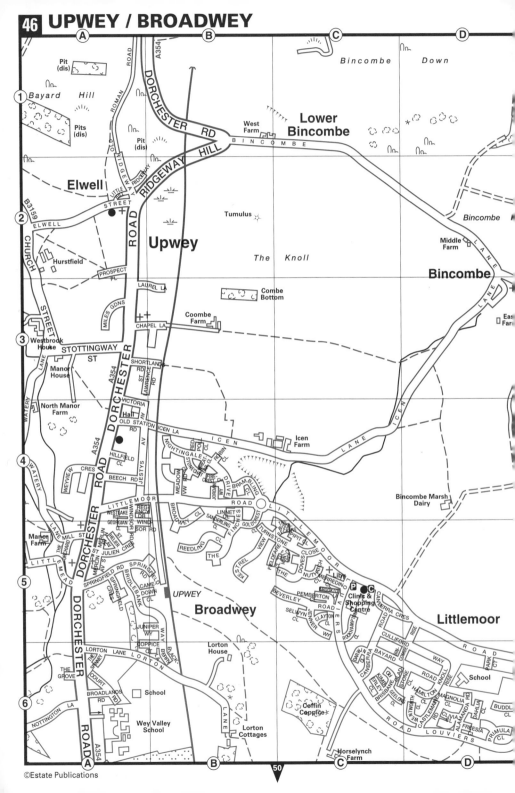

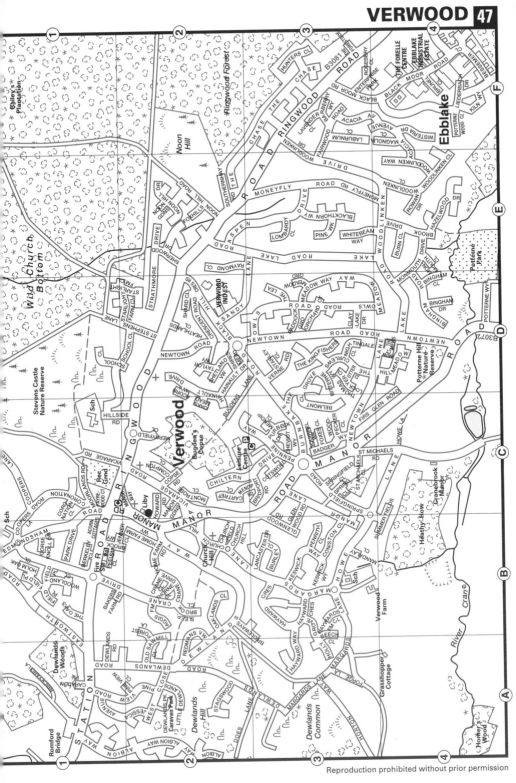

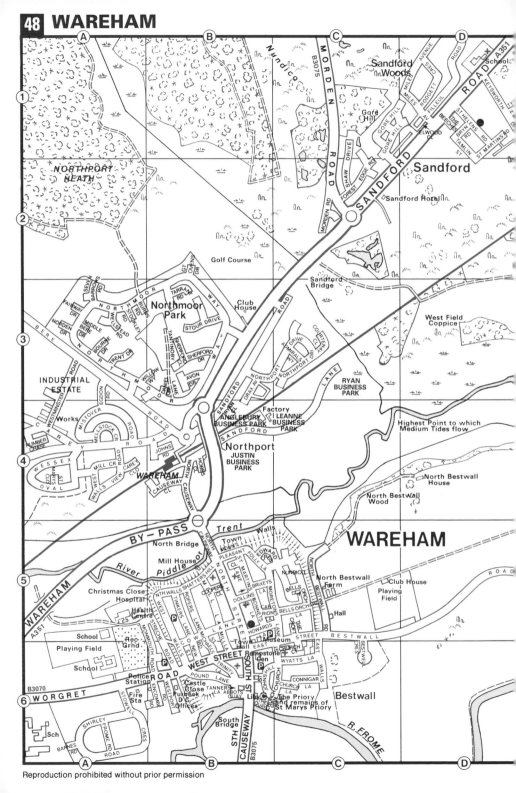

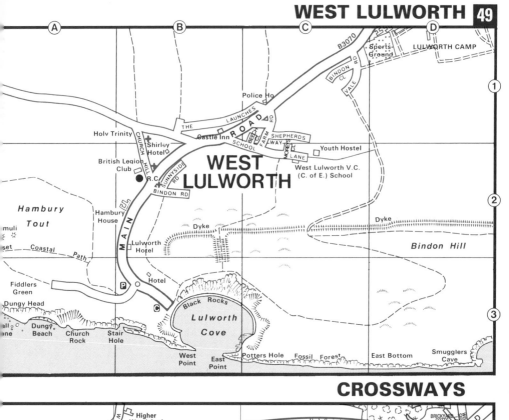

CROSSWAYS

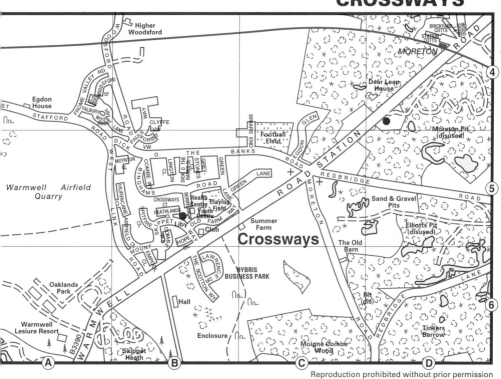

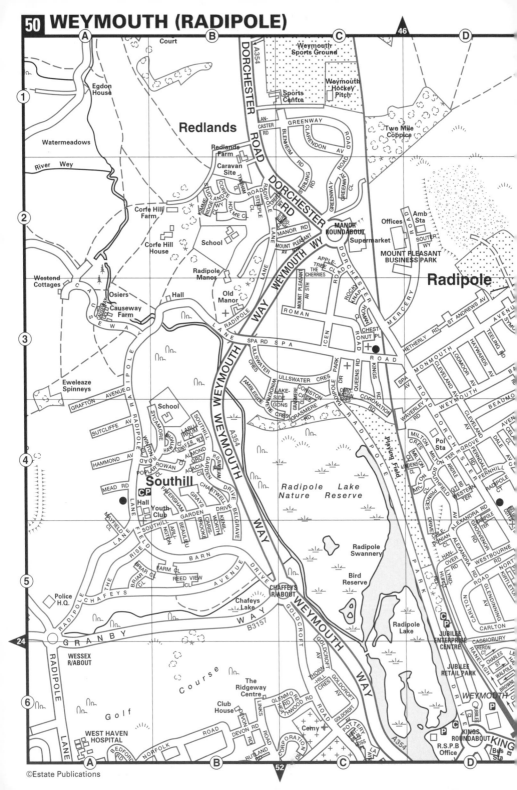

WEYMOUTH (MELCOMBE REGIS) 51

E   F   G   H

Wyke Oliver Farm

WYKE OLIVER
WYKE OLIVER DRIVE

ORCHARD DR
SANGBOURNE RD

A353

WINGREEN CL
MAPLE CL

37

Overcombe

ROAD

FURZY CL

SUNNING-DALE RISE

OVERCOMBE DRIVE

Jordan   Hill

New Barn

ROMAN TEMPLE
(remains of)

C O V E W A Y

Horse Lynch Plantation

AVENUE

KINGSBERE

BODY RD

BODEN LA

CHERRY WY
AVENUE
ELM CL

BUDMOUTH
K-WORTH EN
OAKBURY DRIVE
MELSTOCK AV

EXTON

RINGSTEAD CRES
OVERCOMBE DRIVE

PINE-MOOR CL
MOORDOWN CL
KESTREL MOOR

BRACKENDOWN

AVENUE

EASTDOWN

EASTDOWN CL
HAZELDOWN
EASTDOWN AV

Playground

OAK CL
OAKBURY

FURZY
COVE WAY

HERON CL

PRESTON ROAD

Furzy   Cliff

MOORDOWN
SEA MOOR CL
Wm KOBB

OAKBURY AVENUE

OVERCOMBE

SOUTHDOWN

Hide

BEACHDOWN

AVENUE

WAY

Overcombe Court

SOUTHDOWN AVENUE

*Lodmoor
Nature   Reserve*

BEACHDOWN WAY

PRESTON BEACH ROAD

ESPLANADE   WALK

Waste Centre

A353

B A Y

AVENUE
MOORSIDE AV
MOORSIDE
AVENUE
AVENUE

**Miniature
Golf Course**

P

GREENHILL

**Miniature
Railway**

SPURGE CL
CAMPION CL
LARKSPUR CL

**Sports
Ground**

P

**Aquarium &
Butterfly
Farm**

**Sea Life
Centre**

LYNMOOR
AVENUE

**Melcombe
Regis**

**Model
Village**

P

P.H.

W E Y M O U T H

College

ROWLAND

ROAD

AVENUE   AVENUE

**Weymouth
College**

**Greenhill
Gardens**

ANFORD

COMMUNITY HOSPITAL

**Trimar
Hospice**

MELCOMBE
WESTERHALL ROAD
DORCHESTER RD

GREENHILL

C

GRANGE RD
DORCHESTER RD
SOUTH ST

VICTORIA ST
VICTORIA TER
BRUNSWICK

BELVIDERE

C

Jubilee Clock

E   F   G   H

53

1

2

3

4

5

6

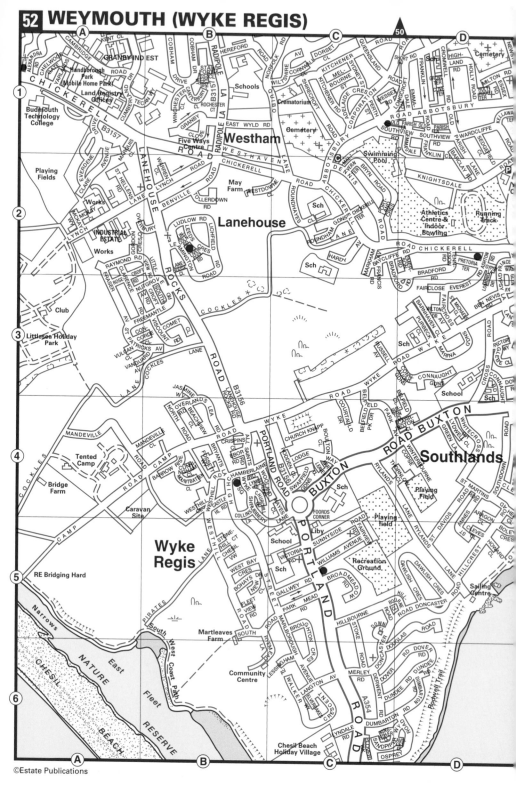

WEYMOUTH

Kings Statue

Seacat Ferry to
Guernsey, Jersey
& St. Malo

Pleasure Pier

Pavilion Theatre

Commercial Pier

Stone Pier

Ferry

The Mixen

Nothe Fort

Old Harbour

Nothe Gardens

Nothe Point

Barracks

CEFAS H.Q.

Newtons Cove

Rodwell

Rodwell Trail

Depot

PORTLAND BREAKWATER

Landing Stage

Landing Stage

Bincleaves Groyne

Ledges

Landing Stage

Western

Landing Stage

Castle Cove

Sandsfoot Castle
(remains of)

PORTLAND HARBOUR

WEYMOUTH BAY

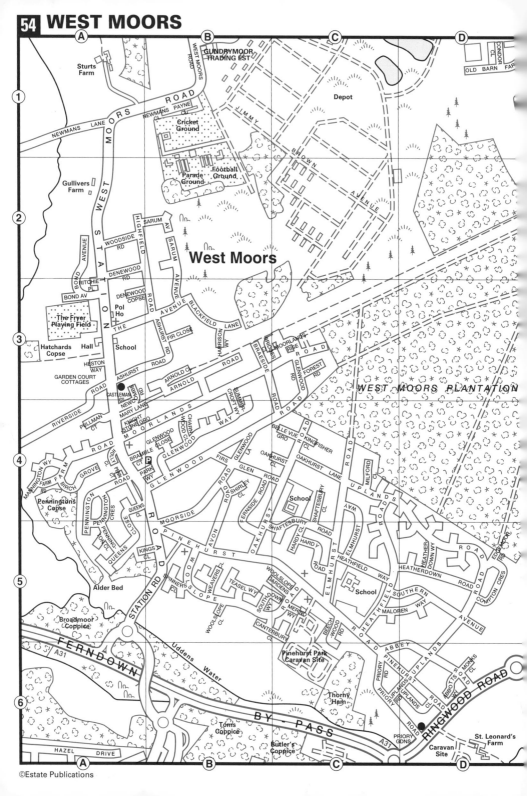

54 WEST MOORS

West Moors

WEST MOORS PLANTATION

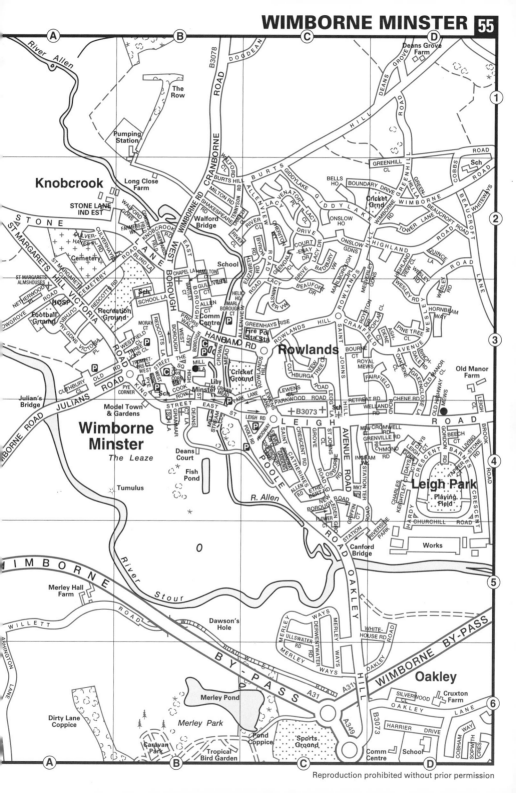

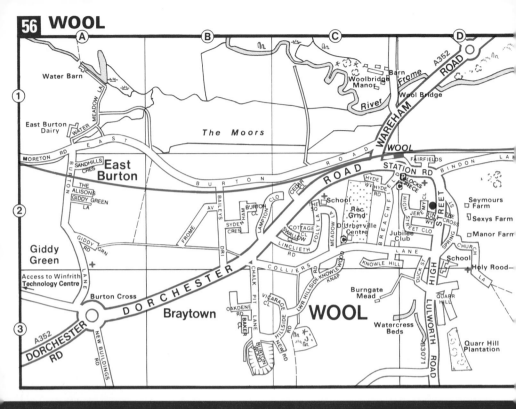

A - Z INDEX TO STREETS
With Postcodes

North Gro DT11　16 D4
Old Bakery Clo DT11　16 A3
Parr Gro DT11　16 A2
Portman Rd DT11　16 A2
Priory Gdns DT11　16 A3
Racedown Rd DT11　16 C3
Rawston Down Rd
DT11　16 C6
St Peters Clo DT11　16 A1
Salisbury Rd DT11　16 A3
School La DT11　16 A2
Snow Down Rd DT11　16 B6
South Cres DT11　16 C4
Stanley Sq ST11　16 D5
Swainson Rd DT11　16 C1
Valley Rd DT11　16 A1
Walters Dri DT11　16 A1
Weiner Clo DT11　16 C5
Yard Farm DT11　16 A3

BLANDFORD FORUM

Albert St DT11　17 B3
Alexandra St DT11　17 B4
Alfred St DT11　17 B4
Andrew Clo DT11　17 D3
Angus Clo DT11　17 C3
Anne Clo DT11　17 C3
Ashmore Clo DT11　17 B2
Avebury Ct DT11　17 B2
Badbury Dri DT11　17 B2
Badgers Sett DT11　17 A6
Balmer Rd DT11　17 C1
Barnes Clo DT11　17 C3
Bayfran Way DT11　17 C4
Beaumont Pk DT11　17 C2
Beckett Clo DT11　17 A6
Beckett Rd DT11　17 A6
Birch Av DT11　17 B6
Black La DT11　17 C4
Blandford Forum
By-Pass DT11　17 A1
Blandford Heights
Ind Est DT11　17 B5
Bournemouth Rd DT11　17 B5
Bryanston St DT11　17 A4
Buttercup La DT11　17 C2
Cadley Clo DT11　17 B3
Carter Clo DT11　17 C3
Casterbridge Clo DT11　17 D2
Castleman Smith Clo
DT11　17 C2
Chapel Gdns DT11　17 C4
Charles St DT11　17 B4
Chettell Way DT11　17 B6
Church La DT11　17 B4
Churchill Rd DT11　17 B3
Cobham Rd DT11　17 B5
Common La DT11　17 B5
Counter Clo DT11　17 D3
Dairy Field DT11　17 D2
Damory Clo DT11　17 B4
Damory Ct St DT11　17 B4
Damory St DT11　17 B4
Davis Gdns DT11　17 C2
Deer Park Rd DT11　17 A4
Dorchester Hill DT11　17 A6
Dorset St DT11　17 B4
Downside Clo DT11　17 C3
Eagle House Gdns
DT11　17 A4
East St DT11　17 B4
East Street La*,
The Close DT11　17 B4
Eastleaze Rd DT11　17 B2
Edward St DT11　17 B4
Elizabeth Rd DT11　17 C3
Fair Mile Rd DT11　17 A6
Fairfield Bungalows
DT11　17 B3
Fairfield Rd DT11　17 B3
Field View Rd DT11　17 C4
Fields Oak DT11　17 B4
Fishers Clo DT11　17 C4
Folly La DT11　17 A6
Forum Mews DT11　17 B4
Froxfield Clo DT11　17 B3
Gent Clo DT11　17 B4
Greenhill Rd DT11　17 B2
Hambledon Gdns
DT11　17 C4
Hanover Ct DT11　17 A4
Harewood Pl DT11　17 B4

Hectors Way DT11　17 A6
Heddington Dri DT11　17 B3
Higher Shaftesbury Rd
DT11　17 B1
Highfields DT11　17 C3
Hilcot Way DT11　17 C3
Hill Rd DT11　17 C2
Hinton Clo DT11　17 B3
Holland Way DT11　17 B3
Holmlea DT11　17 C2
Hunt Rd DT11　17 C3
James Clo DT11　17 D3
Jubilee Way DT11　17 A3
Kings Rd DT11　17 C3
Kingston Clo DT11　17 A3
Kites Corner DT11　17 B1
Knights Clo DT11　17 B6
Kohima Ct DT11　17 B5
Lady Baden Powell Way
DT11　17 C2
Lane Clo DT11　17 D2
Langton Cres DT11　17 C5
Langton Rd DT11　17 B4
Larksmead DT11　17 C2
Letton Clo DT11　17 D1
Lidington Cres DT11　17 B2
Lockeridge Clo DT11　17 B3
Lower School La DT11　17 A6
Manningford Rd DT11　17 B2
Market Pl DT11　17 B5
Marston Clo DT11　17 B3
Martin Clo DT11　17 C3
Mary Cossins Clo
DT11　17 B2
Meadow Vw DT11　17 C5
Medbourne DT11　17 B2
Mellstock Clo DT11　17 D2
Milldown DT11　17 A2
Milldown Rd DT11　17 A1
Mortain Clo DT11　17 B2
New Rd DT11　17 A5
Newman Clo DT11　17 C3
Nordon Rd DT11　17 C3
North Pl DT11　17 B4
Nursery Rd DT11　17 B4
Oakfield St DT11　17 B4
Old Farm Gdns DT11　17 C2
Orchard St DT11　17 B4
Overton Wk DT11　17 B3
Park Lands DT11　17 A4
Park Rd DT11　17 B3
Peel Clo DT11　17 B3
Percy Gdns DT11　17 C4
Phillip Rd DT11　17 C3
Pigeon Clo DT11　17 B6
Pines Ct DT11　17 B4
Pitt Clo DT11　17 B6
Portman Pl DT11　17 A4
Preetz Way DT11　17 D2
Princess Ct DT11　17 B3
Queens Rd DT11　17 B3
Ramsbury Clo DT11　17 B2
Ramsbury Ct DT11　17 B2
Richmond Rd DT11　17 C3
River Mews DT11　17 A4
Riverside Rd DT11　17 C5
Rosebank La DT11　17 C2
Rosefields DT11　17 B6
St Leonards Av DT11　17 C4
St Leonards Ter DT11　17 C3
Salisbury Cres DT11　17 C3
Salisbury Rd DT11　17 B3
Salisbury St DT11　17 B4
Sandbourne Av DT11　17 C2
School La DT11　17 B5
Shaw Clo DT11　17 B3
Sheep Market Hill
DT11　17 B4
Shorts La DT11　17 A4
Shottesford Av DT11　17 C2
Signals Av DT11　17 C2
Southover Clo*,
Birch Av DT11　17 B6
Stanton Clo DT11　17 B3
Station Ct DT11　17 B3
Staverton Walk DT11　17 B3
Stevens Clo DT11　17 C3
Stour Pk DT11　17 B6
Stour Rd DT11　17 C5
The Close DT11　17 C4
The Mount DT11　17 C4
The Orchard DT11　17 A3
The Plocks DT11　17 B4
The Tabernacle*, Sheep
Market Hill DT11　17 B4
Tin Pot La DT11　17 B1

Tudor Gdns DT11　17 D3
Turnpike La DT11　17 A6
Uplands Way DT11　17 B2
Upper School La DT11　17 A6
Vale Pk DT11　17 B5
Victoria Rd DT11　17 B3
Wessex Ct*,
Orchard St DT11　17 B4
West St DT11　17 A5
Wetherbury Clo DT11　17 C1
White Cliff Gdns DT11　17 B4
White Cliff
Mill Hill DT11　17 A2
White Cliff
Mill St DT11　17 B4
Williams Way DT11　17 C2
Wilson Pk DT11　17 C3
Wilverly Gdns DT11　17 C3
Wimborne Rd DT11　17 C4
Windmill Rd DT11　17 C4
Wyvern Way DT11　17 C2

BOURNEMOUTH BOSCOMBE

Adeline Rd BH5　19 G4
Albemarle Rd BH3　18 B1
Albert Rd BH1　18 B5
Alford Rd BH3　18 A1
Alington Rd BH3　18 C2
Alma Rd BH9　18 B1
Alyth Rd BH3　18 A2
Annerley Rd BH1　19 E4
Apsley Ct BH8　18 C3
Arcadia Av BH8　18 D1
Argyll Mansions BH5　19 G4
Argyll Rd BH5　19 G4
Arthur Clo BH2　18 A6
Ascham Rd BH8　18 D3
Ashley Clo BH1　19 G2
Ashley Rd BH1　19 G2
Austin Clo BH1　19 F3
Avenue La BH2　18 B5
Avenue Rd BH2　18 A5
Avon Clo BH8　19 F2
Avon Mews BH8　19 E2
Avon Rd BH8　19 E2
Aylesbury Rd BH1　19 G4
Bath Rd BH1　18 C6
Beacon Rd BH2　18 B6
Beechey Rd BH8　18 C3
Beechwood Av BH5　19 H4
Belgrave Ct BH1　19 F5
Belvedere Rd BH3　19 E2
Bennett Rd BH8　19 E2
Berkeley Rd BH3　18 A1
Berwick Rd BH3　18 B2
Bethany Ho BH1　19 F3
Bethia Clo BH8　19 F2
Bethia Rd BH8　19 F1
Bingham Rd BH9　18 C1
Bishops Clo BH7　19 H1
Bodorgan Rd BH2　18 B4
Bonham Rd BH9　18 B1
Borthwick Rd BH1　19 G3
Boscombe Cliff Rd BH5　19 G5
Boscombe Grove Rd
BH1　19 F3
Boscombe Grove Rd
BH1　19 G3
Boscombe Prom BH5　19 G5
Boscombe Spa Rd BH5　19 F4
Bourne Av BH2　18 A4
Bournemouth Central
Business Pk BH1　19 E3
Bradburne Rd BH2　18 A5
Braidley Rd BH2　18 B5
Branksome Wood Gdns
BH2　18 A4
Branksome Wood Rd
BH2　18 A4
Brompton Ct BH2　18 B5
Browning Av BH5　19 H3
Bryanstone Rd BH3　18 B1
Buchanan Av BH7　19 G2
Burford Ct BH1　19 E5
Byron Rd BH5　19 H4
Cadogan Ct BH1　19 E5
Cambridge Rd BH2　18 A5
Campbell Rd BH1　19 G3
Capstone Pl BH8　19 F2
Capstone Rd BH8　19 F2
Carlton Rd BH1　19 E4
Carnarvon Rd BH1　19 G4

Carysfort Rd BH1　19 F4
Cavendish Hall BH1　18 C3
Cavendish Pl BH1　18 C3
Cavendish Rd BH1　18 C3
Cawdor Rd BH3　18 A1
Cecil Av BH8　19 E1
Cecil Rd BH5　19 G4
Centenary Way BH1　19 G3
Central Dri BH2　18 B4
Charminster Rd BH8　18 C2
Chatsworth Rd BH8　18 D2
Chessel Av BH5　19 H4
Chesterfield Ct BH1　19 E5
Chine Cres BH2　18 A6
Chine Crescent Rd BH2　18 A6
Christchurch Rd BH1　18 D5
Churchill Rd BH1　19 F3
Cleveland Gdns BH1　19 E3
Cleveland Rd BH1　19 F3
Coach House Pl BH1　18 D3
Colman Ct BH1　19 E5
Commercial Rd BH2　18 A5
Corporation Rd BH1　19 E4
Cotlands Rd BH1　18 D4
Courtleigh Manor BH1　19 F4
Crabton Close Rd BH5　19 H4
Cranborne Rd BH2　18 B6
Crescent Rd BH2　18 A5
Crimea Rd BH9　18 B1
Cromer Rd BH8　19 F1
Culford Ct BH8　18 C3
Cumnor Rd*,
Lorne Park Rd BH1　18 C5
Curzon Rd BH1　19 F2
Cyril Rd BH8　19 E2
Dalkeith La*,
Richmond Gdns BH1　18 B5
De Lisle Rd BH3　18 B1
Dean Park Cres BH1　18 C4
Dean Park Rd BH1　18 C4
Derby Rd BH1　19 E4
Donoughmore Rd BH1　19 F4
Dorchester Mansions
BH1　19 F5
Drummond Rd BH1　19 E3
Dunbar Rd BH3　18 B2
Dunkeld Rd BH3　18 A2
Durley Chine BH2　18 A6
Durley Chine Rd BH2　18 A5
Durley Chine Rd Sth
BH2　18 A6
Durley Gdns BH2　18 A6
Durley Rd BH2　18 A6
Durley Rd Sth BH2　18 A6
Durrant Rd BH2　18 B4
East Av BH3　18 A2
East Cliff Prom BH1　18 C6
East Overcliff Dri BH1　18 C6
Egerton Gdns BH8　19 F2
Egerton Rd BH8　19 F2
Elgin Rd BH4　18 A1
Elwyn Rd BH1　19 E3
Erinbank Mansions
BH1　19 E5
Exbourne Manor BH1　19 E5
Exeter Cres BH2　18 B5
Exeter La BH2　18 B5
Exeter Park Rd BH2　18 B6
Exeter Rd BH2　18 B5
Fairhaven Ct BH5　19 G4
Fenwick Ct BH8　18 D3
Fir Vale Rd BH1　18 C5
Fitzharris Av BH9　19 C1
Florence Rd BH5　19 G4
Fortescue Rd BH3　18 C2
Frances Rd BH1　19 E4
Gainsborough Rd BH7　19 H1
Garden Ct BH1　19 F1
Garfield Av BH1　19 F2
Gerald Rd BH3　18 C2
Gervis Pl BH1　18 B5
Gervis Rd BH1　18 C5
Gilbert Rd BH8　19 F2
Gladstone Rd BH7　19 H3
Gladstone Rd West
BH1　19 G3
Glen Fern Rd BH1　18 C5
Glen Rd BH5　19 G4
Glencoe Rd BH7　19 H1
Glenferness Av BH4　18 A1
Gloucester Rd BH7　19 H2
Gordon Rd BH1　19 F4
Gorsecliff Ct BH5　19 G4
Grafton Clo BH3　18 C1
Grafton Rd BH3　18 C1
Grange Ct BH1　18 D5

Grantham Rd BH1　19 G3
Grantley Rd BH5　19 H4
Grants Av BH1　19 F2
Grants Clo BH1　19 G2
Granville Pl*,
Yelverton Rd BH1　18 B5
Green Pk BH1　19 F5
Grosvenor Ct BH5　19 H3
Grosvenor Gdns BH1　19 G4
Grove Rd BH1　18 C5
Grovely Av BH5　19 H4
Hahnemann Rd BH2　18 A6
Hamilton Clo BH1　19 F3
Hamilton Rd BH1　19 F3
Harewood Av BH7　19 H1
Harewood Cres BH7　19 H1
Harewood Gdns BH7　19 H1
Harrison Av BH1　19 F2
Haviland Mews*,
Haviland Rd BH2　19 H3
Haviland Rd BH7　19 H3
Haviland Rd East BH7　19 H3
Haviland Rd West*,
Ashley Rd BH1　19 H3
Hawkwood Rd BH5　19 G2
Hayes Av BH7　19 G2
Heathcote Rd BH5　19 H4
Hengist Rd BH1　19 F4
Henville Rd BH8　19 E3
Heron Court Rd BH3　18 C1
Hinton Rd BH1　18 C5
Holdenhurst Rd BH8　18 C3
Homedale Ho BH1　18 C3
Horace Rd BH5　19 G4
Howard Rd BH1　19 E1
Huntly Rd BH3　18 B2
Ibsley Clo BH8　19 F2
Iddesleigh Rd BH3　18 B2
Jefferson Av BH1　19 F2
Kensington Dri BH2　18 A4
Kerley Rd BH2　18 B6
Keswick Rd BH5　19 H4
Keverstone Ct BH1　19 F5
Kings Park Central Dri
BH7　19 G2
Kings Park Dri BH7　19 G2
Kings Park Rd BH7　19 G2
Kings Rd BH3　18 C1
Kinross Rd BH3　18 A2
Knole Ct BH1　19 F4
Knole Gdns BH1　19 F4
Knole Rd BH1　19 F3
Knyveton Ho BH1　19 E4
Knyveton Rd BH1　19 E4
Langton Rd BH1　19 H3
Lansdowne Cres*,
Lansdowne Rd BH1　18 D5
Lansdowne Gdns BH1　18 C4
Lansdowne Rd BH1　18 C3
Lansdowne Rd Sth
BH1　18 D4
Lawrence Ct BH8　19 E2
Leamington Rd BH9　19 E1
Leeson Rd BH7　19 G1
Leven Av BH4　18 A4
Lincoln Av BH1　19 F2
Linwood Rd BH9　18 D1
Little Forest Rd BH4　18 A2
Littledown Av BH7　19 G1
Littledown Dri BH7　19 G1
Lonsdale Rd BH3　18 B1
Lorne Park Rd BH1　18 C5
Lowther Gdns BH8　19 E3
Lowther Rd BH8　18 C2
Lytton Rd BH1　19 E3
Madeira Rd BH1　18 C5
Madison Av BH1　19 F2
Malmesbury Ct BH8　19 E2
Malmesbury Park Pl
BH8　19 E3
Malmesbury Park Rd
BH8　18 D2
Mannington Pl*,
West Hill Rd BH2　18 A5
Manor Rd BH1　19 E4
Marina Clo BH5　19 G5
Marina Rd BH5　19 G5
Marina Twrs BH5　19 G5
Marwell Clo BH7　19 H1
Maxwell Rd BH9　18 C1
Melbourne Rd BH8　19 E3
Merlewood Clo BH2　18 B3
Mermaid Ct BH5　19 G5
Methuen Clo BH8　19 E2
Methuen Rd BH8　19 E2
Meyrick Park Cres BH3　18 B2

Meyrick Rd BH1 18 D5
Michelgrove Rd BH5 19 G5
Milton Rd BH8 18 C3
Moorland Rd BH1 19 F4
Mount Stuart Rd BH5 19 G5
Myrtle Rd BH8 19 F2
Nairn Rd BH3 18 B2
North Rd BH7 19 G3
Northcote Rd BH1 19 E4
Nortoft Rd BH8 18 D2
Norwich Av BH2 18 A5
Norwich Av West BH2 18 A5
Norwich Rd BH2 18 A5
Oak Rd BH8 19 E2
Oban Rd BH3 18 B1
Ocean Heights BH8 19 H5
Old Christchurch La*,
  Old Christchurch Rd
  BH1 18 C5
Old Christchurch Rd
  BH1 18 B5
Ophir Gdns BH8 19 E3
Ophir Rd BH8 18 D3
Orchard St BH2 18 B5
Orcheston Rd BH8 19 E2
Owls Rd BH5 19 F5
Oxford Rd BH8 19 F5
Palmerston Mews BH1 19 G3
Palmerston Rd BH1 19 G3
Park Rd BH8 18 D4
Parker Rd BH9 18 B1
Parsonage Rd BH1 18 C5
Pegasus Ct BH1 18 C3
Percy Rd BH5 19 G4
Pier App BH2 18 C6
Pine Mansions BH1 19 G5
Poole Hill BH2 18 A5
Portchester Ct BH8 18 D3
Portchester Pl BH8 18 D3
Portchester Rd BH8 18 C2
Portman Rd BH7 19 H3
Post Office Rd BH1 18 B5
Priory Rd BH2 18 B6
Purbeck Rd BH2 18 A5
Queens Gdns BH2 18 A4
Queens Pk Gdns BH8 19 F1
Queens Pk Rd BH8 19 F1
Queens Pk South Dri BH8 19 F2
Queens Pk West Dri BH8 19 E1
Queens Rd BH2 18 A4
Randolph Rd BH1 19 G4
Richmond Bridge Rd BH8 19 F2
Richmond Gdns BH1 18 B5
Richmond Hill BH2 18 B5
Richmond Hill Dri BH2 18 B4
Richmond Park Av BH8 18 D1
Richmond Park Clo*,
  Holdenhurst Rd BH8 19 F2
Richmond Park Cres BH8 19 E1
Richmond Park Rd BH8 18 D1
Richmond Wood Rd BH8 18 D1
Roslin Rd BH3 18 B1
Roslin Rd Sth BH3 18 A1
Ross Glades BH3 18 B2
Roumelia La BH5 19 G4
Royal Arc BH1 19 G4
Rushton Cres BH3 18 B2
Russell Cotes Rd BH1 18 C5
St Albans Av BH8 18 D1
St Albans Rd BH8 18 D1
St Anns Ct*,
  Palmerston Mews BH1 19 G3
St Anthonys Rd BH2 18 B3
St Augustins Rd BH2 18 B3
St Clements Gdns BH1 19 F3
St Clements Rd BH1 19 F3
St Davids Ct*,
  Palmerston Mews BH1 19 G3
St Georges Ct*,
  Palmerston Mews BH1 19 G3
St Ives Gdns BH2 18 C3
St James Sq BH5 19 H3
St Johns Ct*,
  Palmerston Mews BH1 19 G3
St Johns Rd BH5 19 G4
St Ledgers Pl BH8 19 F2
St Ledgers Rd BH8 19 F1

St Leonards Rd BH8 18 D2
St Lukes Rd BH3 18 B1
St Marys Rd BH8 19 F2
St Michaels Mew*,
  West Hill Rd BH2 18 A5
St Michaels Pl*,
  West Hill Rd BH2 18 A5
St Michaels Rd BH2 18 A5
St Pauls La BH8 18 D4
St Pauls Pl BH8 18 D4
St Pauls Rd BH8 18 D4
St Peters Cres*,
  St Peters Rd BH1 18 C5
St Peters Rd BH1 18 C5
St Stephens Rd BH2 18 B4
St Stephens Way BH2 18 B4
St Swithuns Rd BH1 18 D4
St Swithuns Rd Sth BH1 18 D4
St Valerie Rd BH2 18 B3
St Winifreds Rd BH2 18 B3
Salisbury Rd BH1 19 G4
San Remo Twrs BH5 19 G5
Sandringham Ct BH8 19 E2
Sea Rd BH5 19 G5
Shaftesbury Rd BH8 19 E2
Shelbourne Rd BH8 18 D2
Shelbourne Rd BH8 19 F2
Shelley Clo BH1 19 G3
Shelley Gdns BH1 19 G3
Shelley Rd BH1 19 G3
Shelley Rd East BH7 19 G3
Silchester Clo BH2 18 B4
Soberton Rd BH8 19 F1
Somerset Rd BH7 19 H3
Somerville Rd BH2 18 A5
South Rd,
  Boscombe BH1 18 C6
South Rd,
  Bournemouth BH1 19 G3
South View Pl BH2 18 A5
Southcote Rd BH1 19 E4
Sovereign Centre BH1 19 G3
Spencer Rd BH1 19 E4
Spring Rd BH1 19 E3
Stafford Rd BH1 18 D5
Stanley Rd BH1 19 E3
Stewart Clo BH8 19 E3
Stewart Rd BH8 18 D2
Stirling Rd BH3 18 A1
Stoke Wood Rd BH3 18 B2
Stour Rd BH8 19 F2
Suffolk Rd BH2 18 A5
Suffolk Rd Sth BH2 18 A4
Surrey Rd BH2, BH4 18 A4
Talbot Av BH3 18 A1
Talbot Rd BH9 18 B1
Tamworth Rd BH7 19 H3
Temple Mews BH1 19 F2
Terrace Mount BH2 18 B5
Terrace Rd BH2 18 B5
The Albany BH1 19 E5
The Charltons BH2 18 B3
The Crescent BH1 19 G4
The Deans BH1 19 C4
The Firs BH1 18 C4
The Lane BH8 19 E3
The Marina BH5 19 G5
The Point BH5 19 G5
The Square BH2 18 B5
The Triangle BH2 18 A5
Thistlebarrow Rd BH7 19 G2
Tower Rd BH1 19 G3
Trafalgar Rd BH9 18 C1
Tregonwell Rd BH2 18 B5
Trinity Rd BH1 18 C4
Truscott Av BH9 18 C1
Undercliff Dri BH1 18 C6
Undercliff Rd BH5 19 G5
Upper Hinton Rd BH1 18 C5
Upper Norwich Rd BH2 18 A5
Upper Terrace Rd BH2 18 B5
Vale Mansions BH1 19 F4
Vale Rd BH1 19 F4
Verulam Pl*,
  Yelverton Rd BH1 18 B5
Victoria Pl BH1 19 E3
Victoria Rd BH1 19 E3
Walpole Rd BH1 19 F3
Washington Av BH1 19 F2
Waterloo Rd BH9 18 B1
Watkin Rd BH5 19 H4
Waverley Rd BH8 18 D3
Wellington Ho BH8 18 D3
Wellington Rd BH1 18 C2
Wesley Clo BH8 19 E3

Wessex Way BH8 18 A4
West Cliff Gdns BH2 18 A6
West Cliff Prom BH2 18 B6
West Cliff Rd BH2 18 A6
West Hill Pl*,
  West Hill Rd BH2 18 A6
West Hill Rd BH2, BH4 18 A5
West Overcliff Dri BH4 18 A6
West Undercliff Prom BH2 18 A6
Westby Rd BH5 19 G4
Weston Dri BH1 18 D5
Westover Rd BH1 18 C5
Wharncliffe Rd BH5 19 F4
Wilfred Rd BH5 19 H4
William Rd BH7 19 G1
Wilson Rd BH1 19 F2
Wilton Rd BH7 19 H3
Wimborne Rd BH3, BH2 18 B2
Windermere Rd BH3 18 C1
Windham Mews BH1 19 F3
Windham Rd BH1 19 F3
Windsor Rd BH5 19 G4
Wingfield Ct BH1 19 E5
Wollstonecraft Rd BH5 19 H4
Wolverton Rd BH7 19 H3
Woodford Rd BH1 19 E4
Wooton Mount Gdns BH1 18 C5
Wootton Mount BH1 18 C5
Wychwood Clo BH2 18 B4
Wychwood Dri BH2 18 B3
Yelverton Rd BH1 18 B5
York Rd BH1 18 D4

BOVINGTON CAMP

Alamein Rd BH20 22 D5
Amiens Rd BH20 22 B4
Andover Grn BH20 22 A5
Arras Cres BH20 22 B4
Arras Rd BH20 22 B4
Balaclava Rd BH20 22 B4
Bony Rd BH20 22 C4
Bovington La BH20 22 B6
Cachy Rd BH20 22 B5
Capper Rd BH20 22 B5
Cologne Rd BH20 22 B5
Cranesmoor Clo BH20 22 A5
Cunningham Clo BH20 22 D5
Duncan Cres BH20 22 D5
8th August Rd BH20 22 B4
Elles Rd BH20 22 A4
Erin Rd BH20 22 B4
Foxbury Rd BH20 22 A4
Framerville Rd BH20 22 B4
Gaza Rd BH20 22 B4
Gouzeaucourt Rd BH20 22 B4
Heath Clo BH20 22 A4
Higher Wood BH20 22 B5
Holt Rd BH20 22 A4
King George V Rd BH20 22 B4
Linsay Rd BH20 22 B4
Lower Cranesmoor BH20 22 A5
Morris Rd BH20 22 D5
New Rd BH20 22 B4
Purbeck View Rd BH20 22 B4
Rhine Rd BH20 22 B5
Robertson Rd BH20 22 A4
Ross Clo BH20 22 C5
St Julien Rd BH20 22 B4
Sewell Rd BH20 22 A4
Sir Richard Hull Rd BH20 22 A5
Swinton Av BH20 22 B4
Victoria Clo BH20 22 B5
Wain Rd BH20 22 A4
Windsor Clo BH20 22 B5

BRIDPORT BOTHENHAMPTON

Acer Av DT6 20 E2
Alexandra Ct DT6 21 B5
Alexandra Rd DT6 20 B4
Allington Gdns DT6 20 A2
Allington Mead DT6 20 B2
Allington Pk DT6 20 B3
Armstrong Rd DT6 20 C2
Arrowfield DT6 20 B4
Asker Gdns DT6 20 D4
Asker Mead DT6 20 D4
Banton Shard DT6 20 C1
Barrack Rd DT6 20 C4
Bath Orchard DT6 20 F1
Beaminster Rd DT6 20 E1
Beaumont Av DT6 20 D3
Bedford Pl DT6 20 C3
Bedford Ter DT6 20 C3
Blind La Clo DT6 20 F1
Bothen Dri DT6 20 D4
Bowhayes DT6 20 D4
Bramble Dri DT6 21 C7
Bramley Hill DT6 20 E2
Brit View Rd DT6 21 A7
Broad La DT6 21 A5
Broadmead Av DT6 20 B3
Burton Rd DT6 21 C6
Buttercup Way DT6 21 C7
Caley Way DT6 20 F2
Castle Sq DT6 20 C4
Chancery La*,
  Folly Mill La DT6 20 C4
Chards Mead Rd DT6 20 C3
Cherrytree La DT6 20 A2
Cherrytrees DT6 20 B2
Chestnut Rd DT6 21 C6
Church Clo DT6 20 F1
Church St DT6 20 C4
Claremont Gdns DT6 20 D2
Claremont Rd DT6 20 D2
Coneygar Clo DT6 20 C2
Coneygar La DT6 20 C2
Coneygar Rd DT6 20 C2
Coopers Dri DT6 21 D6
Corbin Way DT6 20 E1
Cordover Gdns DT6 20 D4
Coronation Rd DT6 20 B4
Court Clo DT6 20 F1
Court Orchard Rd DT6 20 B2
Crock La DT6 21 D5
Dark La DT6 21 B5
Delapre Rd DT6 20 D3
Diments Sq DT6 20 B2
Dodhams Farm Clo DT6 20 E1
Dodhams La DT6 20 D1
Donkey La DT6 20 B2
Dottery Rd DT6 20 B2
Downes St DT6 20 C4
Dreadnought Trading Est DT6 20 B4
Drew Clo DT6 20 E3
Duck St DT6 21 D6
East Rd DT6 20 D4
East St DT6 20 C4
Edgehill Rd DT6 21 B5
Elizabeth Av DT6 21 B5
Elwell DT6 21 D5
Esplanade DT6 21 B8
First Cliff Walk DT6 21 A8
Fishweir La DT6 20 E1
Fishweir Fields DT6 20 E2
Fishweir Rd DT6 20 E1
Flaxhayes DT6 20 C2
Flood La DT6 21 C5
Folly Mill Gdns DT6 20 D4
Folly Mill La DT6 20 C4
Forsters La DT6 20 C2
Forty Foot Way DT6 21 B8
Foundry Clo DT6 20 B4
Foundry La DT6 20 B4
Fouracre Clo DT6 20 C2
Fourth Cliff Walk DT6 21 A8
Fox Clo DT6 20 F2
Foxglove Way DT6 21 C7
Fulbrooks Clo DT6 20 B3
Fulbrooks La DT6 20 B3
Gale Cres DT6 20 B4
Garden Clo DT6 20 C3
George St DT6 21 C8
Gladstone Clo DT6 20 E3
Glebe Clo DT6 21 D5
Gore Cross Way DT6 20 F1
Gore La DT6 20 F1
Green Clo DT6 20 E2
Green La,
  Walditch DT6 20 F3
Green La,
  Bothenhampton DT6 21 D5
Gundry La DT6 20 C4
Gundry Rd DT6 20 A3
Gypsy La DT6 20 D1

Happy Island Way DT6 20 E3
Hardy Rd DT6 20 D3
Hemlets Clo DT6 20 E1
Hibernia Pl DT6 20 B2
Higher St DT6 20 F1
Hill Clo DT6 21 B8
Hill Rise DT6 21 B8
Hillingdon DT6 20 E2
Hillview DT6 20 E1
Hillview Estate DT6 20 B2
Hollow Way DT6 21 C5
Hospital La DT6 20 B2
Howard Clo DT6 20 F3
Howard Rd DT6 20 E4
Jessopp Av DT6 20 D3
Journeys End DT6 20 B4
Kenwyn Rd DT6 20 D3
King Charles Way DT6 20 F3
King St DT6 20 D4
King William Head DT6 20 E1
Kings Head DT6 20 E1
Kingsnorth Clo DT6 20 E3
Knightstone Rise DT6 20 E2
Lake La DT6 21 D6
Lansdowne Rd DT6 21 C6
Laurel Clo DT6 20 B2
Lee La DT6 20 F3
Long La,
  Bothenhampton DT6 21 E6
Longs La,
  Bridport DT6 20 D3
Lower Walditch La DT6 20 E4
Magdalane La DT6 20 B4
Main St DT6 21 D6
Manor Fields DT6 21 D6
Maple Gdns DT6 21 C5
Marrowbone La DT6 21 E6
Marsh Barn Rd DT6 21 C8
Marsh Gate DT6 21 C7
Mead Flds DT6 20 B2
Mead La DT6 20 A2
Meadow Ct DT6 20 C4
Meadowlands DT6 21 C7
Meadway DT6 21 A8
Meech Clo DT6 21 D6
Middle St DT6 20 F1
Mount Pleasant DT6 20 B3
Mountjoy DT6 21 C6
Nordons DT6 21 D5
Norman Clo DT6 20 E3
Normandy Way DT6 20 C4
North Allington DT6 20 B2
North Hill Way DT6 21 C6
North Mills Rd DT6 20 C3
North Mills Trading Est DT6 20 C2
North St DT6 20 C2
Nursery Gdns DT6 20 D3
Old Church Rd DT6 21 D6
Old Laundry Trading Est DT6 20 D3
Orchard Av DT6 20 C2
Orchard Cres DT6 20 B2
Osbourne Rd DT6 20 F1
Pageant Clo DT6 20 F1
Park Rd DT6 20 B3
Parsonage Rd DT6 20 D3
Pasture Way DT6 21 D5
Pier Ter DT6 21 B8
Pine Vw DT6 20 B4
Plumtree Gdns DT6 20 D4
Poppy Way DT6 21 C7
Princess Rd DT6 21 B5
Priory La DT6 20 C4
Pymore Rd DT6 20 C2
Pymore Ter DT6 20 D1
Quarry La DT6 21 D6
Quayside DT6 21 B8
Queens Av DT6 20 B4
Queenswell DT6 20 D1
Rax La DT6 20 C3
Rendalls Walk DT6 20 C4
Ridgeway DT6 20 E1
Rope Walk DT6 20 C4
Ropers Ct DT6 20 C4
Roundham Gdns DT6 21 C6
St Andrews Cres DT6 20 D3
St Andrews La DT6 20 E2
St Andrews Ind Est DT6 20 E2
St Andrews Rd DT6 20 D3
St Cecilia's Gdns DT6 20 C2

St James Park DT6 20 F1
St Katherines Av DT6 20 D3
St Katherines Dri DT6 20 E2
St Lukes Ct DT6 20 A2
St Michaels Ind Est
DT6 20 B4
St Michaels La DT6 20 B4
St Swithins Av DT6 20 B3
St Swithins Rd DT6 20 B3
Sea Rd Nth DT6 20 D4
Sea Rd Sth DT6 21 C5
Seaward Gdns DT6 21 C7
Second Cliff Walk DT6 21 A8
Shoe La DT6 20 E2
Simene Clo DT6 20 A3
Skilling Hill Rd DT6 21 B5
Slades Green DT6 21 D5
South Lawns DT6 21 D5
South Mill La DT6 21 C5
South St DT6 20 C4
South Walk DT6 20 C4
Sparacre Gdns DT6 20 C3
Spring Clo DT6 20 E1
Station Rd DT6 21 C8
Stuart Way DT6 20 E3
Suttil Cres DT6 20 D1
Tannery Rd DT6 20 B4
Third Cliff Walk DT6 21 A8
Thomson Clo DT6 20 B3
Thread Mill La DT6 20 D1
Townsend Way DT6 20 E1
Trinity Way DT6 20 F1
Trustin Clo DT6 20 B2
Uplands DT6 20 F4
Valley Rd DT6 21 D6
Vearse Clo DT6 21 B5
Victoria Gro DT6 20 C3
Village Rd DT6 20 F1
Walditch Rd DT6 20 E4
Wanderwell DT6 21 C6
Warne Hill DT6 20 D2
Watton Gdns DT6 20 D2
Watton La DT6 21 A5
Watton Park DT6 21 B5
Wellfields Dri DT6 20 E2
West Allington DT6 20 B3
West Bay Rd DT6 21 C5
West Cliff DT6 21 A8
West Gables Clo DT6 20 A3
West Mead DT6 20 A3
West Rd DT6 20 A3
West St DT6 20 B3
West Walk DT6 21 A7
White Clo DT6 20 F2
Willow Way DT6 20 E3
Wych Hill DT6 21 C7
Wych Ridge DT6 21 C7
Wychside Clo DT6 21 D7

BROADMAYNE WEST KNIGHTON

Bakers Paddocks DT2 15 C6
Beech Clo DT2 15 B6
Bramble Drove DT2 15 B6
Bramble Edge DT2 15 B5
Broadmead DT2 15 B5
Chalky Rd DT2 15 A6
Charlmont Cross DT2 15 C6
Charlmont Ct*,
   Main St DT2 15 B5
Conway Dri DT2 15 B5
Cowleaze Rd DT2 15 B6
Cross Trees Clo DT2 15 B6
Glebe Way DT2 15 C4
Hardys Row DT2 15 C4
High Trees DT2 15 C6
Knighton La DT2 15 C5
Lewell Way DT2 15 C4
Littlemead DT2 15 B6
Main St DT2 15 B5
Martel Clo DT2 15 A6
Oakwood DT2 15 C4
Old Brickfields DT2 15 C5
Osmington Drove DT2 15 B6
Rectory Clo DT2 15 B6
Rectory Rd DT2 15 B6
St Martins Clo DT2 15 B5
Sherren Cotts DT2 15 C6
South Drove DT2 15 A6
South Vw DT2 15 C5
Spring Gdns DT2 15 C5
Stafford Clo DT2 15 C4
The Spinney DT2 15 B6

Watergates La DT2 15 C5
Woodlands DT2 15 B6

BURTON BRADSTOCK

Annings La DT6 22 B2
Barr La DT6 22 B2
Barrowfield Clo DT6 22 B2
Beach Rd DT6 22 C3
Bindbarrow Rd DT6 22 C3
Bredy Rd DT6 22 C2
Burton Rd DT6 22 A1
Chapel St DT6 22 B2
Charles Rd DT6 22 B2
Church St DT6 22 B2
Cliff Rd DT6 22 B3
Common La DT6 22 B3
Darby La DT6 22 B2
Grove Orchard DT6 22 B2
Grove Rd DT6 22 B2
High St DT6 22 B2
Hive Clo DT6 22 C3
Lower Townsend DT6 22 B1
Mill St DT6 22 B2
Norburton DT6 22 C1
North Hill Clo DT6 22 C1
Northover Clo DT6 22 C1
Shadrach DT6 22 B2
Shipton La DT6 22 B1
South Annings DT6 22 B1
Southover DT6 22 B3

CHARMINSTER

Broken Cross DT2 23 D3
Brook Clo DT2 23 C1
Church La DT2 23 C2
Charlotte Clo DT2 23 D3
Cocklands DT2 23 C3
Down End DT2 23 D2
East Hill DT2 23 C2
Ellerslie Clo DT2 23 C2
Gascoyne La DT2 23 A3
Greenacre DT2 23 C2
Higher Charminster
DT2 23 C1
Highfield Clo DT2 23 B1
Hill Vw DT2 23 B2
Meadow View DT2 23 B3
Mill La DT2 23 C1
North St DT2 23 C1
Pound Clo DT2 23 B2
Sodern La DT2 23 A2
Symonds Ct DT2 23 D3
The Square DT2 23 C2
Vicarage Clo DT2 23 C2
Vicarage Gdns DT2 23 C2
Vicarage La DT2 23 D2
Wanchard La DT2 23 B1
Weir View DT2 23 B2
West Hill DT2 23 B2
Westleaze DT2 23 D3
Westleaze Clo DT2 23 D3
York Clo DT2 23 C2

CHARMOUTH

Axminster Rd DT6 23 A4
Barneys Clo DT6 23 C4
Barrs La DT6 23 C4
Bridge Rd DT6 23 D4
Charberry Rise DT6 23 A5
Double Common DT6 23 B5
Downside Clo DT6 23 B5
Ellesdon DT6 23 D4
Five Acres DT6 23 B5
Gardenside DT6 23 B5
Georges Clo DT6 23 C4
Greenhayes DT6 23 A5
Hammonds Mead DT6 23 B5
Higher Sea La DT6 23 B4
Kidmore Clo DT6 23 B5
Lower Sea La DT6 23 C6
Meadow Way DT6 23 C5
Nutcombe Clo DT6 23 A4
Old Lyme Hill DT6 23 A4
Old Lyme Rd DT6 23 A4
Old Rectory Clo DT6 23 C5
Orchard Clo DT6 23 B5

Parkway DT6 23 C5
Queens Walk DT6 23 C4
River Way DT6 23 C5
St Andrews Dri DT6 23 B4
The Street DT6 23 B4
Wesley Clo DT6 23 C4
We'stcliff Rd DT6 23 A5

CHICKERELL

Albany Rd DT4 24 D3
Aldabrand Clo DT3 24 C2
Avocet Clo DT3 24 B2
Avon Clo DT4 24 D3
Bakehouse Corner*,
   Garston Hill DT3 24 A1
Browns Cres DT3 24 C2
Cambridge Rd DT4 24 D3
Chickerell Rd DT3 24 A1
Cumberland Dri DT4 24 D3
Curlew Clo DT3 24 B2
Drake Av DT3 24 C2
East St DT3 24 B1
Elziver Clo DT3 24 B3
Fairfield DT3 24 C2
Fishermans Clo DT3 24 C1
Fleet La DT3 24 A2
Fleet Rd DT3 24 A2
Garston Hill DT3 24 A1
Glennie Way DT3 24 C3
Granby Ind Est DT4 24 D3
Grebe Clo DT3 24 C2
Green La DT3 24 C2
Hampshire Rd DT4 24 D3
Heron Clo DT3 24 C2
Higher End DT3 24 B1
Lerrett Clo DT3 24 C1
Lower Putton La DT3 24 C1
Lower Way DT3 24 B1
Lugger Clo DT3 24 A1
Mariners Way DT3 24 B1
Marshallsay Ct DT3 24 B1
Marshallsay Rd DT3 24 B1
Maskew Clo DT3 24 B2
May Ter Gdns DT3 24 B1
Meadow Clo DT3 24 C3
Mohune Way DT3 24 C2
North Sq DT3 24 B1
Plover Dri DT3 24 C2
Podington Mdws DT3 24 C1
Pugmill La DT3 24 C2
Putton La DT3 24 C2
Randall Clo DT3 24 B1
Rashley Rd DT3 24 B1
Rex La DT3 24 B2
Rolfe Cres DT3 24 B1
School Clo DT3 24 C1
School Hill DT3 24 C1
Spiller Rd DT3 24 B2
Surrey Clo DT4 24 D3
Teal Av DT3 24 B2
The Bindells DT3 24 C2
The Coppice DT3 24 C1
The Hythe DT3 24 C2
The Knapp DT3 24 A1
The Stalls DT3 24 A1
Trenchard Way DT3 24 A1
West Clo DT3 24 A1
West St DT3 24 A1
Wheat Farland DT3 24 C1
Whynot Way DT3 24 B2
Wilmslow Rd DT3 24 B1

CHRISTCHURCH

Addington Pl BH23 26 D4
Addiscombe Rd BH23 26 A3
Airfield Ind Est BH23 27 F4
Airfield Rd BH23 27 F4
Airfield Way BH23 27 F3
Airspeed Rd BH23 27 G3
Alder Clo BH23 26 C1
Alexander Clo BH23 26 C1
Ambassador Clo BH23 27 G4
Ambassador Ind Est
BH23 27 F4
Ambury La BH23 27 E3
Amethyst Rd BH23 27 E3
Amsterdam Sq BH23 26 C4
Anchor Clo BH23 27 G4
Andover Rd BH23 27 H3
Anne Clo BH23 26 A1

Anson Clo BH23 27 F4
Argyle Rd BH23 27 E5
Ariel Clo BH6 26 B6
Ariel Dri BH6 26 B6
Arthur La BH23 26 A3
Arthur Rd BH23 26 A3
Asquith Clo BH23 26 D5
Auster Clo BH23 27 G3
Avenue Rd BH23 26 A2
Avon Bldgs BH23 26 A2
Avon Rd East BH23 26 A2
Avon Run Clo BH23 27 G5
Avon Run Rd BH23 27 G5
Avon Trading Pk BH23 26 A3
Avon Wharf BH23 26 C4
Baldwin Clo BH23 26 D4
Bank Clo BH23 26 B4
Bargates BH23 26 A3
Baring Rd BH6 26 A6
Barrack Rd BH23 26 A3
Batten Clo BH23 26 D3
Beaconsfield Rd BH23 26 B3
Beauchamp Pl BH23 26 A3
Beaufort Clo BH23 27 H3
Beaver Ind Est BH23 27 F4
Belfield Rd BH6 26 A6
Bellflower Clo BH23 27 G2
Belvedere Rd BH23 26 A3
Beresford Gdns BH23 27 E4
Bingham Clo BH23 27 E3
Bingham Rd BH23 26 D3
Blackberry La BH23 27 E4
Blenheim Dri BH23 27 G4
Bluebell Clo BH23 27 H2
Bodowen Clo BH23 26 D1
Bodowen Rd BH23 26 D1
Bonington Clo BH23 27 E3
Brabazon Dri BH23 27 G3
Braemar Av BH6 26 A6
Braemar Clo BH6 26 A6
Branders Clo BH6 26 A6
Branders La BH6 26 A5
Branwell Clo BH23 26 A1
Briar Clo BH23 27 E4
Bridge St BH23 26 C4
Britannia Way BH23 27 G4
Broadway BH6 26 A6
Bronte Av BH23 26 A1
Brook Way BH23 27 H3
Bub La BH23 27 H3
Buccaneers Clo BH23 26 D4
Burdock Clo BH23 27 H1
Bure Clo BH23 27 H4
Bure Haven Dri BH23 27 G4
Bure Homage Gdns
   BH23 27 G4
Bure Homage La
   BH23 27 G4
Bure La BH23 27 G5
Bure Pk BH23 27 H4
Bure Rd BH23 27 H4
Burton Clo BH23 26 C1
Burton Rd BH23 26 D3
Buttercup Dri BH23 27 G1
Caledonian Clo BH23 27 H3
Calkin Clo BH23 26 A2
Cameron Rd BH23 26 D3
Campion Gro BH23 27 E4
Capesthorne BH23 27 E5
Caroline Av BH23 27 E5
Carradale BH23 27 H2
Castle St BH23 26 B4
Catalina Clo BH23 27 G4
Caxton Clo BH23 27 F3
Celandine Clo BH23 27 H2
Centenary Ho BH23 26 A3
Chant Clo BH23 26 D3
Charles Rd BH23 27 F2
Charlotte Clo BH23 27 F4
Cheviot Clo BH23 26 D4
Chichester Way BH23 27 G5
Chiltern Ct*,
   Hunt Rd BH23 27 D5
Christchurch By-Pass
   BH23 26 B3
Church La BH23 26 B4
Church St BH23 26 B4
Clarendon Rd BH23 26 A3
Clematis Clo BH23 27 H2
Cliff Dri BH23 27 H4
Clover Clo BH23 27 H2
Coastguard Way BH23 27 E6
Coleridge Grn BH23 27 F3
Columbine Clo BH23 27 H1
Comet Way BH23 27 G4
Cornflower Dri BH23 27 H1

Cotswold Ct*,
   Hunt Rd BH23 27 D5
Court Clo BH23 26 D4
Creedy Dri BH23 26 B5
Creedy Path BH23 26 B4
Cricket Clo BH23 27 F5
Cringle Av BH6 26 A6
Croft Rd BH23 27 F3
Cunningham Clo BH23 27 F4
Curlew Rd BH23 27 F4
Dairy Clo BH23 26 D4
Dakota Clo BH23 27 G3
De Havilland Way
   BH23 27 F5
Delft Mews*,
   Scotts Hill La BH23 26 D4
Delta Clo BH23 27 G3
Dennistoun Av BH23 27 E3
Deverel Clo BH23 26 A2
Disraeli Rd BH23 26 D4
Donnington Dri BH23 27 H3
Dorset Rd BH23 27 E2
Drake Clo BH23 27 F4
Draper Rd BH23 27 E3
Druitt Rd BH23 27 E2
Ducking Stool La
   BH23 26 B4
Dunecliff Rd BH6 26 A6
Dunlin Clo BH23 27 G5
Edward Rd BH23 27 F2
Elderberry La BH23 27 F4
Emily Clo BH23 26 A1
Everest Rd BH23 26 D2
Fairfield BH23 26 B3
Fairfield Clo BH23 26 B3
Fairmile Rd BH23 26 A2
Falcon Dri BH23 27 F5
Farm La BH23 27 F5
Fishermans Bank BH23 27 E5
Flambard Av BH23 26 A1
Fountain Way BH23 26 B4
Foxglove Clo BH23 27 H2
Foxwood Av BH23 27 E5
Friars Rd BH23 27 G4
Frobisher Clo BH23 27 F4
Fulmar Rd BH23 27 G5
Gladstone Clo BH23 26 D4
Gleadowe Av BH23 26 A4
Glendale Rd BH6 26 A6
Glengarry Way BH23 27 F4
Gordon Way BH23 26 C1
Grafton Clo BH23 26 D4
Grange Rd BH23 27 G3
Grange Rd Business
Centre BH23 27 G3
Grebe Clo BH23 27 F4
Green Acres BH23 27 F3
Grove Rd East BH23 26 A2
Groveley Rd BH23 27 F4
Haarlem Mews BH23 26 C3
Haking Rd BH23 26 D3
Halifax Way BH23 27 G3
Hamilton Clo BH23 27 G4
Harbour Cres BH23 27 E5
Harbour View Ct*,
   Queens Rd BH23 26 D5
Hardy Clo BH23 26 D3
Hawkins Clo BH23 27 F5
Haworth Clo BH23 26 A1
Hawthorn Rd BH23 27 E2
High St BH23 26 B4
Highcliffe Rd BH23 27 G2
Hillary Rd BH23 27 E2
Hoburne La BH23 27 H2
Holly Gdns BH23 26 D1
Honeybourne Cres
   BH6 26 A6
Honeysuckle Way
   BH23 27 G2
Howard Clo BH23 27 F5
Howe Clo BH23 27 F5
Hughes Business
Centre BH23 27 F3
Hunt Rd BH23 27 E2
Hunter Clo BH23 27 F4
Hynesbury Rd BH23 27 H4
Inveravon BH23 27 F6
Irvine Way BH23 27 E2
Island View Av BH23 27 G4
Jellicoe Clo BH23 27 F4
Johnstone Rd BH23 27 E4
Kay Clo BH23 27 E4
Kenilworth Ct*,
   Stour Rd BH23 26 A3
Kestrel Dri BH23 27 G4
Keyes Clo BH23 27 F4

Kingfisher Way BH23 27 F5
Kings Av BH23 26 A4
Kingsley Av BH6 26 A6
Kingsley Clo BH6 26 A6
Knapp Clo BH23 26 A2
Knapp Mill Av BH23 26 A2
Knowles Clo BH23 26 D3
Ladysmith Clo BH23 26 D3
Lancaster Clo BH23 27 H3
Lark Rd BH23 27 G4
Latch Farm Av BH23 26 A2
Le Patourel Clo BH23 26 D3
Ledbury Rd BH23 27 E5
Leyside BH23 27 F3
Lights Clo BH23 26 A3
Lineside BH23 26 C2
Lingwood Av BH23 27 E4
Livingstone Rd BH23 26 D3
Lyndhurst Rd BH23 27 G2
Lysander Clo BH23 26 A4
Magdalen La BH23 26 A4
Magnolia Clo BH6 26 A5
Mallard Clo BH23 27 F4
Mallory Clo BH23 27 F2
Mallow Clo BH23 27 H2
Malmesbury Clo BH23 26 A5
Malvern Ct*,
  Dorset Rd BH23 27 C5
Manor Rd BH23 26 A4
Marabout Clo BH23 26 D3
Marina Vw BH23 26 A5
Mariners Ct BH23 27 F4
Marmion Grn BH23 27 E3
Marsh Clo BH23 26 A4
Marsh La BH23 26 D4
Martins Hill Clo BH23 26 C1
Martins Hill La BH23 26 C1
Masterson Clo BH23 26 D3
Meadowland BH23 27 E4
Medlar Clo BH23 26 D1
Mendip Ct*,
  Dorset Rd BH23 27 C5
Meredith Clo BH23 26 D3
Merlin Way BH23 27 G5
Mill Rd BH23 26 A2
Miller Rd BH23 26 D3
Millhams St BH23 26 B4
Millhams St Nth BH23 26 B4
Minterne Rd BH23 27 E5
Moffat Rd BH23 26 D3
Monkshood Clo BH23 27 H1
Monkswell Grn BH23 26 C4
Mortimer Clo BH23 27 G4
Mountbatten Clo BH23 27 F5
Mude Gdns BH23 27 F5
Mudeford BH23 27 E5
Mudeford Green Clo
  BH23 27 F5
Mudeford La BH23 26 D4
Nelson Dri BH23 27 F4
Newcroft Gdns BH23 26 A2
Newlands Rd BH23 27 F3
Normandy Dri BH23 26 D3
Norton Clo BH23 26 D3
Nugent Rd BH6 26 A6
Orchard Clo BH23 26 A4
Orchard Mews BH23 26 A4
Orchid Way BH23 26 C3
Osprey Clo BH23 27 F5
Palmerston Av BH23 26 D4
Park Gdns BH23 27 E3
Partridge Clo BH23 27 F5
Pauntley Rd BH23 27 E4
Pelham Clo BH23 26 D4
Pennant Way BH23 27 F3
Pennine Ct*,
  Hunt Rd BH23 27 D6
Peregrine Rd BH23 27 F5
Pinehurst Av BH23 27 F5
Pipers Dri BH23 27 G3
Poppy Clo BH23 27 H2
Portfield Clo BH23 26 A3
Portfield Rd BH23 26 A3
Primrose Way BH23 27 H2
Princess Av BH23 26 B5
Priory Ct BH23 26 B5
Priory Ind Pk BH23 27 G3
Priory Quay BH23 26 B5
Promenade BH23 27 H4
Promenade BH23 27 H5
Purbeck Ct*,
  Dorset Rd BH23 27 D5
Purewell BH23 26 C4
Purewell Clo BH23 26 D4
Purewell Ct BH 26 D3

Purewell Cross Rd
  BH23 26 C3
Quantock Ct*,
  Hunt Rd BH23 27 D6
Quay Rd BH23 26 B4
Queens Av BH23 26 B5
Queens Rd BH23 26 D4
Raleigh Clo BH23 27 F5
Raven Way BH23 27 F5
Redvers Rd BH23 26 D3
Regency Cres BH23 26 A2
Regent Way BH23 26 B4
Reid St BH23 26 A3
Ricardo Cres BH23 27 G4
Rimbury Way BH23 26 A2
Riverdale La BH23 26 A4
Riverlea Rd BH23 26 A4
Riversdale Rd BH6 26 A6
Riverside Pk BH23 26 A5
Robin Gdns BH23 26 A3
Robins Way BH23 27 G5
Rodney Ct BH23 27 F4
Rodney Dri BH23 27 F4
Roeshott Hill BH23 27 H1
Rook Hill Rd BH23 27 H4
Roscrea Clo BH6 26 B6
Roscrea Dri BH6 26 B6
Rosedale Clo BH23 27 E4
Rossiters Quay BH23 26 C4
Rotterdam Dri BH23 26 C4
Rushford Warren BH23 27 F5
Russell Dri BH23 26 D4
Saffron Dri BH23 27 G2
St Johns Rd BH23 26 A4
St Margarets Av BH23 26 A5
Salisbury Rd BH23 26 D1
Sandown Rd BH23 27 E4
Sandy Plot BH23 26 C2
Sarah Sands Clo BH23 26 D2
Saxon Centre BH23 26 B4
Saxon King Gdns BH6 26 A6
Saxon Sq BH23 26 B4
Saxonford Rd BH23 27 H4
Scotts Grn BH23 27 F2
Scotts Hills La BH23 26 D4
Sea Vixen Ind Est
  BH23 27 F3
Seafield Rd BH23 27 H4
Seaway Av BH23 27 H3
Sheldrake Rd BH23 27 G5
Sherwood Clo BH23 26 A3
Shorts Clo BH23 26 C1
Silver Business Pk
  BH23 27 E3
Silver St BH23 26 B4
Slinn Rd BH23 27 E3
Smugglers Reach
  BH23 27 F5
Snowdrop Gdns BH23 27 H2
Somerford Av BH23 27 G2
Somerford
  Business Pk BH23 27 F3
Somerford Rd BH23 27 F3
Somerford Way BH23 27 E3
Sopers La BH23 26 A4
Sopwith Clo BH23 27 G4
Sorrell Ct BH23 27 G2
Sorrell Way BH23 27 G2
South View Rd BH23 26 A4
Southcliffe Rd BH23 27 H4
Southdown Ct*,
  Dorset Rd BH23 27 C5
Southey Rd BH23 27 E2
Speedwell Dri BH23 27 G2
Springfield Av BH6 26 A6
Springwater Dri BH23 26 D4
Stanpit BH23 26 D4
Staplecross La BH23 26 D2
Station Rd BH23 26 A3
Stirling Way BH23 27 G4
Stonechat Ct BH23 27 E3
Stony La BH23 26 C1
Stony La South BH23 26 C4
Stour Rd BH23 26 A5
Stourbank Rd BH23 26 A4
Strete Mount BH23 27 E3
Stroud Gdns BH23 27 E4
Stroud La BH23 27 E4
Stroud Park Av BH23 27 E4
Summers La BH23 26 D1
Sunderland Dri BH23 27 H3
Sundew Clo BH23 27 H1
Swan Grn BH23 26 A5
Swordfish Dri BH23 27 G3
Tangmere Clo BH23 27 G4
Tensing Rd BH23 26 D2

The Buttery BH23 26 D3
The Coppice BH23 27 G4
The Hawthorns BH23 27 E4
The Runway BH23 27 H3
Thornbury Rd BH6 26 A6
Tidemill Clo BH23 26 A2
Tilburg Rd BH23 26 C4
Trafalgar Ct BH23 27 F5
Treebys Clo BH23 26 D1
Trefoil Way BH23 27 H2
Troak Clo BH23 26 D2
Twynham Av BH23 26 A4
Valiant Way BH23 27 G3
Vecta Clo BH23 27 H4
Verwood Cres BH6 26 A6
Vetch Clo BH23 27 H2
Vickery Way BH23 26 D3
Victoria Rd BH23 27 E5
Viking Clo BH6 26 A6
Viking Way,
  Mudeford BH23 27 G5
Viking Way,
  Wick BH6 26 A6
Villette Clo BH23 26 A1
Viscount Dri BH23 27 G4
Vulcan Way BH23 27 G3
Warren Av BH23 27 F5
Watermead BH23 26 A5
Watermill Rd BH23 26 A2
Waterside BH23 27 E6
Watery La BH23 27 F1
Wellesley Av BH23 27 H3
Wenlock Ct*,
  Hunt Rd BH23 27 D5
Wessex Clo BH23 27 H3
West Clo BH6 26 A6
West View Rd BH23 26 D4
Westfield Gdns BH23 27 G2
Whimbrel Ct BH23 27 F4
Whitehall BH23 26 B5
Whitehayes Rd BH23 26 C1
Wick La,
  Christchurch BH23 26 B5
Wick La, Wick BH6 26 A5
Wick Point Mws BH23 26 B5
Wickfield Av BH23 26 B4
Wickfield Clo BH23 26 B4
Wicklea Rd BH6 26 B6
Wickmeads Rd BH6 26 A6
Wildfell Clo BH23 26 A1
Willow Dri BH23 26 A5
Willow Pl BH23 26 B4
Willow Way BH23 26 A5
Wilverley Rd BH23 27 F3
Winston Ct*,
  Stour Rd BH23 26 A3
Wolfe Clo BH23 26 D3
Woodruff Clo BH23 27 H2
Wren Clo BH23 27 G5
Yarrow Clo BH23 27 H2

CORFE CASTLE

Abbotts Cotts BH20 24 B5
Battlemead BH20 24 C5
Calcraft Rd BH20 24 C5
Colletts Clo BH20 24 C6
East St BH20 24 B4
Halves Cotts BH20 24 B6
Higher Filbank BH20 24 C6
Higher Gdns BH20 24 C5
Hollands Clo BH20 24 B5
Jubilee Gdns BH20 24 C6
Market Sq BH20 24 B4
Mead Rd BH20 24 C6
Mohune Way BH20 24 C3
Sandy Hill La BH20 24 C4
Springwell Clo BH20 24 B5
The Bindells BH20 24 C3
The Dollings BH20 24 C6
Tilbury Mead BH20 24 C6
Townsend Mead BH20 24 C6
Townsend Rd BH20 24 C6
Webbers Clo BH20 24 B5
West St BH20 24 B4

CORFE MULLEN

Abbotsbury Rd BH18 25 D3
Albert Rd BH21 25 B3
Amber Rd BH21 25 A4
Anvil Cres BH18 25 D3

Ascot Rd BH18 25 E3
Banstead Rd BH18 25 F3
Barry Gdns BH18 25 E3
Barters La BH18 25 D4
Beech Clo BH18 25 C4
Berwyn Ct BH18 25 F4
Birch Clo BH21 25 B2
Birdale Ct BH18 25 E3
Birkdale Rd BH18 25 F3
Blacksmith Clo BH21 25 B3
Blandford Rd BH21 25 C1
Blaney Way BH21 25 B2
Blythe Rd BH21 25 B2
Bognor Rd BH18 25 E4
Broadmoor Rd BH21 25 A2
Broadstone Way BH18 25 E4
Brook La BH21 25 A2
Brookdale Clo BH18 25 F3
Brookdale Farm BH18 25 F3
Brownsea Av BH21 25 C2
Buddens Mdw BH21 25 A4
Caesars Way BH18 25 C3
Cecil Clo BH21 25 D2
Central Av BH21 25 B1
Chapel Clo BH21 25 B1
Chapel La BH21 25 A3
Cheam Rd BH18 25 D4
Clarendon Clo BH18 25 E3
Clarendon Rd BH18 25 D4
Colin Clo BH21 25 C1
Corfe Lodge Rd BH18 25 C4
Corfe View Rd BH21 25 B3
Cotton Clo BH18 25 E3
Courtney Pl BH21 25 B3
Coventry Clo BH21 25 A4
Croft Clo BH21 25 B1
Dairy Clo BH21 25 A4
Dalkeith Rd BH21 25 C4
Dell Clo BH18 25 D4
Dennis Rd BH21 25 C3
Diana Way BH21 25 D1
Diprose Rd BH21 25 C1
Dunyeats Rd BH18 25 F4
East Way BH21 25 C3
Erica Dri BH21 25 B2
Fairview Cres BH18 25 E3
Fairview Dri BH18 25 F3
Fairview Rd BH18 25 E3
Firside Rd BH21 25 B4
Froud Way BH21 25 B4
George Rd BH21 25 C1
Georges Mews BH21 25 C1
Gladelands Clo BH18 25 C4
Gladelands Way BH18 25 C4
Golf Links Rd BH18 25 F3
Gorse Rd BH21 25 A3
Grange Rd BH18 25 F4
Gurney Rd BH21 25 C2
Hamilton Rd BH21 25 C3
Hanham Rd BH21 25 C3
Hartnell Ct BH21 25 B3
Haven Rd BH21 25 B2
Haywards La BH21 25 B1
Hazeldene BH18 25 D2
Heather Clo BH21 25 D1
Heckford Rd BH21 25 B3
Henbury Clo BH21 25 C2
Henbury Rise BH21 25 B3
Henbury View Rd
  BH21 25 B2
Heysham Rd BH18 25 F4
High Park Rd BH18 25 D3
High Way BH18 25 E4
Higher Blandford Rd
  BH21 25 D1
Highfield Clo BH21 25 C3
Highfield Rd BH21 25 C4
Highmoor Clo BH21 25 C3
Highmoor Rd BH21 25 C3
Hill View Ct BH21 25 B3
Hillcrest Rd BH21 25 B3
Hillside Gdns BH21 25 A4
Hillside Mews BH21 25 B4
Hillside Rd BH21 25 A4
Hillside Way BH21 25 B3
Hilltop Rd BH21 25 C2
Holland Way BH21 25 D3
Insley Cres BH18 25 D3
Ivor Rd BH21 25 C2
Jacklin Ct BH18 25 F3
Jubilee Clo BH21 25 D1
Jubilee Rd BH21 25 C1
Kiln Clo BH21 25 A4
Kirkway BH18 25 F4
Knoll La BH21 25 A2
Lancaster Clo BH18 25 D3

Lancaster Dri BH18 25 D3
Laurel Clo BH21 25 B2
Lewesdon Dri BH18 25 D4
Link Rise BH21 25 C2
Lower Blandford Rd
  BH18 25 F4
Lower Golf Links Rd
  BH18 25 F3
Macaulay Rd BH18 25 B4
Marian Clo BH21 25 B4
Marian Rd BH21 25 B4
Meadow Rise BH18 25 D3
Moor Rd BH18 25 F3
Moorside Rd BH21 25 B3
Oak Clo BH21 25 B3
Orchard Clo BH21 25 B1
Orchard La BH21 25 B1
Phelips Rd BH21 25 C1
Primrose Way BH21 25 C1
Pye Clo BH21 25 C1
Queens Rd BH21 25 C1
Ralph Rd BH21 25 C1
Ridgeway BH18 25 F4
Roman Heights BH21 25 C1
Roman Rd BH18 25 C1
Rushcombe Way BH21 25 C2
St Andrews Rd BH18 25 F3
Silverdale Clo BH18 25 C4
South Rd BH21 25 C2
Southlands Av BH21 25 C2
Southlands Clo BH21 25 C2
Southlands Ct.. BH18 25 F4
Springdale Av BH18 25 E3
Springdale Gro BH21 25 C4
Springdale Rd BH18 25 B4
Station App BH18 25 F4
Story La BH18 25 F4
Sunningdale Gdns
  BH18 25 E3
Sutherland Av BH18 25 D3
Terence Rd BH21 25 B3
The Close BH18 25 C4
The Parade BH21 25 B3
Thornton Clo BH21 25 B3
Tower Farm BH21 25 C1
Towers Way BH21 25 C1
Troon Rd BH18 25 F3
Tudor Rd BH18 25 F3
Upton Way BH18 25 D4
Victoria Clo BH21 25 B3
Viewside Clo BH21 25 B3
Wareham Rd BH21 25 A4
Warland Way BH21 25 C1
Waterloo Rd BH21 25 A2
Wayman Rd BH21 25 D2
Wentworth Dri BH18 25 F3
West Way BH18 25 E4
Westheath Rd BH18 25 F4
Wickham Dri BH21 25 C4
Widworthy Dri BH18 25 E3
Willis Clo BH21 25 C4
Windgreen BH21 25 C1
Wyatts Clo BH21 25 B2
Wyatts La BH21 25 B2
Wynne Clo BH18 25 D4
York Rd BH18 25 F4

CROSSWAYS

Airfield Clo DT2 49 B5
Berrylands DT2 49 B5
Binghams Rd DT2 49 B5
Briars End DT2 49 C4
Brackyard Cotts DT2 49 D4
Clyffe View DT2 49 B4
Combe Way DT2 49 B5
Crossways Ct DT2 49 B5
Dick O the Banks Clo
  DT2 49 B5
Dick O the Banks Rd
  DT2 49 B5
Egdon Glen DT2 49 C5
Empool Clo DT2 49 B6
Forest View DT2 49 B5
Frome Valley Rd DT2 49 A4
Green La DT2 49 B5
Grey Stones Clo DT2 49 B5
Heathlands Clo DT2 49 B5
Hope Clo DT2 49 B5
Hurricane Clo DT2 49 B5
Hybris Business Pk
  DT2 49 C6
Lawrence Dri DT2 49 B6
Lington Clo DT2 49 B5

St Georges Estate Rd DT5 31 B6
St Georges Rd DT5 31 C6
St Johns Clo DT5 30 C3
St Martins Rd DT5 30 B3
St Pauls Rd DT5 30 C3
Sea Vw DT5 30 B3
Sharpits DT5 31 B6
Shepherds Croft DT5 31 E5
Shortlands DT5 31 C8
Southwell Rd DT5 31 C8
Spring Gdns DT5 30 B3
Station Rd DT5 31 C6
Straits DT5 31 D6
The Grove DT5 31 F5
Three Yards Clo DT5 30 B3
Tilleycoombe Rd DT5 30 C3
Tobys Clo DT5 31 B7
Tradecroft DT5 31 B5
Tradecroft Ind Est DT5 31 B5
Ventnor Rd DT5 30 B3
Verne Common Rd DT5 30 B2
Verne Rd DT5 30 C3
Victoria Pl DT5 31 C5
Victoria Rd DT5 31 E5
Victoria Sq DT5 30 B2
Victory Rd DT5 30 B2
Vindelis Ct DT5 30 B2
Wakeham DT5 31 D6
Wallsend Clo DT5 31 B8
Weare Clo DT5 30 B4
West Gro Ter DT5 31 E5
Westcliff Rd DT5 31 B7
Weston Rd DT5 31 B7
Weston St DT5 31 B7
Wide St DT5 31 B5
Withies Croft DT5 31 F5
Woolcombe Rd DT5 31 A7
Yeats Rd DT5 30 C3
Yeolands Rd DT5 31 B7

GILLINGHAM

Abbotts Way SP8 32 B3
Addison Clo SP8 32 C5
Arun Clo SP8 32 B2
Avondale Gdns SP8 32 B2
Barley Fields SP8 32 B1
Barnaby Mead SP8 32 B4
Bay Fields SP8 32 B3
Bay La SP8 32 C3
Bay Rd SP8 32 B3
Black Lawn SP8 32 C2
Bourne Way SP8 32 B2
Briar Clo SP8 32 A3
Brickfields Business Pk SP8 32 C5
Brickyard La*, New M SP8 32 C5
Bridge Clo SP8 32 D5
Broad Robin SP8 32 A4
Brookside SP8 32 C2
Buckingham Rd SP8 32 B4
Byrony Gdns SP8 32 A3
Campion Clo SP8 32 A3
Casterbridge Way SP8 32 A2
Cemetery Rd SP8 32 B3
Chaffinch Way SP8 32 C5
Cherryfields SP8 32 B2
Chestnut Way SP8 32 A4
Church View SP8 32 B4
Church Walk SP8 32 B4
Claremont Av SP8 32 B2
Cloverfield SP8 32 B2
Coldharbour SP8 32 A3
Common Mead Av SP8 32 B4
Common Mead La SP8 32 A5
Cordery Gdns SP8 32 B2
Coronation Rd SP8 32 B3
Cypress Way SP8 32 B3
Davenant Clo SP8 32 A4
Deane Av SP8 32 A4
Deweys Way SP8 32 B2
Dolphin La SP8 32 B2
Downsview Dri SP8 32 B2
Edith Ct SP8 32 B2
Fairey Clo SP8 32 A4
Fairey Cres SP8 32 B2
Fairybridge SP8 32 B2

Fern Brook La SP8 32 D5
Floramour Way*, Cypress Way SP8 32 B3
Foxglove Clo SP8 32 A3
Great House Walk SP8 32 B3
Gyllas Way SP8 32 B2
Ham Ct SP8 32 D5
Hanover La SP8 32 A4
Hardings La SP8 32 C4
Hardy Ct SP8 32 A2
Hawthorn Av SP8 32 A3
Heatherfields SP8 32 B2
High St SP8 32 B4
Highgrove SP8 32 B2
Himar Clo SP8 32 A4
Hine Clo SP8 32 D5
Honeyfields SP8 32 B2
Horsefields SP8 32 B2
Hyde Rd SP8 32 A3
Iris Gdns SP8 32 A4
Ivy Clo SP8 32 A3
Jay Walk SP8 32 D5
Jesop Clo SP8 32 A4
Juniper Gdns SP8 32 A4
King Edmund Ct SP8 32 B3
King John Rd SP8 32 D4
Kingfisher Av SP8 32 D5
Kings Court Clo SP8 32 D4
Kingsgourt Rd SP8 32 D5
Knoll Pl SP8 32 B2
Laburnam Way SP8 32 A5
Lammas Clo SP8 32 B2
Lawrence Cotts SP8 32 C5
Le Neubourg Way SP8 32 B4
Leddington Way SP8 32 A2
Lockwood Ter SP8 32 D5
Lodbourne Grn SP8 32 B3
Lodbourne Ter SP8 32 B3
Lodden View SP8 32 C5
Maple Way SP8 32 A4
Marlott Rd SP8 32 A2
Mathews Pl SP8 32 A3
Meadowcroft SP8 32 C5
Melchester SP8 32 B2
Melstock Rd SP8 32 A2
Mill Race SP8 32 B3
Mulberry Clo SP8 32 C3
New Rd SP8 32 C5
Newbury SP8 32 C4
Newton Clo SP8 32 A4
Orchard Rd SP8 32 B3
Palace Rd SP8 32 D4
Paris Ct SP8 32 B4
Peacemarsh SP8 32 B2
Peacemarsh Farm Clo SP8 32 B2
Pheasant Way SP8 32 D6
Pimpernel Ct SP8 32 A3
Poppyfields Rd SP8 32 A3
Primrose Clo SP8 32 A3
Purns Mill La SP8 32 B1
Queen Eleanor Rd*, Palace Rd SP8 32 D4
Queen St SP8 32 B3
Railway Ter SP8 32 C4
Regency Ct*, Stuart La SP8 32 A4
River View SP8 32 A3
Rolls Bridge La SP8 32 A3
Rolls Bridge Way SP8 32 A3
Roman Business Centre*, Le Neubourg Way SP8 32 B3
Rookery Clo SP8 32 D5
Rose Ct SP8 32 C4
St Martins Sq SP8 32 B3
St Marys Ct SP8 32 B4
Saxon Mead Clo SP8 32 B2
School La SP8 32 C4
School Rd SP8 32 C4
Shaftesbury Rd SP8 32 C5
Shreen Clo SP8 32 C3
Shreen Way SP8 32 C3
Somerset Clo SP8 32 B2
South St SP8 32 B4
Sparrow Croft SP8 32 D5
Station Rd SP8 32 C5
Stour Ct SP8 32 A3
Stour Gdns SP8 32 A4
Stour Meadows SP8 32 A4
Stourcastle Clo SP8 32 A2
Stuart La SP8 32 A4
Sutton Clo SP8 32 A4
Sycamore Way SP8 32 A4
Sydney Pl SP8 32 A4

Sylvan Clo SP8 32 C2
Sylvan Way SP8 32 B2
The Laurels SP8 32 A4
The Meadows SP8 32 C5
The Oaks SP8 32 A4
The Square SP8 32 A4
Thurstin Way SP8 32 B2
Tomlins La SP8 32 B3
Trent Sq SP8 32 D5
Turners La SP8 32 B3
Victoria Rd SP8 32 C4
Wavering La E SP8 32 A3
Wavering La W SP8 32 A3
Waverland Ter SP8 32 B3
Weatherbury Rd SP8 32 A2
Wessex Way SP8 32 A2
Whitehouse Ct*, Tomlins La SP8 32 B3
Wiltshire Clo SP8 32 A2
Woodpecker Mdw SP8 32 D5
Woodsage Dri SP8 32 A3
Wyke Rd SP8 32 A3

HAMWORTHY

Albany Gdns BH15 45 E4
Aldis Gdns BH15 45 D3
Almer Rd BH15 45 C2
Annett Clo BH15 45 D3
Ashmore Av BH15 45 E4
Ashmore Cres BH15 45 E4
Beccles Clo BH15 45 E4
Beckhampton Rd BH15 45 D2
Benjamin Rd BH15 45 C3
Blandford Clo BH15 45 E4
Blandford Rd BH15, BH16 45 C1
Bransea Av BH15 45 C4
Bransea Clo BH15 45 D4
Burngate Rd BH15 45 D4
Carisbrooke Cres BH15 45 C2
Carmel Clo BH15 45 D4
Carters Av BH15 45 C1
Caversham Clo BH15 45 D3
Cobbs Quay BH15 45 E2
Coles Av BH15 45 D4
Coles Gdns BH15 45 D3
David Way BH15 45 C3
Dawkins Rd BH15 45 D2
Dean Clo BH15 45 D2
Delilah Rd BH15 45 C3
Eccles Rd BH15 45 F3
Egmont Rd BH15 45 A2
Elijah Clo BH15 45 D3
Falconer Dri BH15 45 D1
Fitzworth Av BH16 45 B2
Foreland Rd BH16 45 A1
Fort Cumberland Clo BH15 45 C3
Freshwater Dri BH15 45 D1
Galloway Rd BH15 45 C2
Goathorn Clo BH15 45 C1
Goliath Rd BH15 45 D3
Halter Path BH15 45 D3
Hamilton Clo BH15 45 D3
Hamilton Cres BH15 45 D3
Hamilton Rd BH15 45 D3
Harkwood Dri BH15 45 D2
Hercules Rd BH15 45 C3
Hewitt Rd BH15 45 D1
Hinchcliffe Clo BH15 45 E3
Hinchcliffe Rd BH15 45 E3
Hounslow Clo BH15 45 D4
Hoyal Rd BH15 45 C4
Inglesham Way BH15 45 D4
Ivor Rd BH15 45 F4
Jacobs Rd BH15 45 C3
Joshua Clo BH15 45 D3
Junction Rd BH16 45 B2
Kangaw Pl BH15 45 C4
Keysworth Rd BH16 45 B1
Lake Av BH15 45 C4
Lake Cres BH15 45 D3
Lake Dri BH15 45 C4
Lake Rd BH15 45 C4
Legion Clo BH15 45 D4
Legion Rd BH15 45 D4
Lulworth Av BH15 45 D4
Lulworth Clo BH15 45 D4
Lulworth Cres BH15 45 C4
Manton Clo BH15 45 D2
Manton Rd BH15 45 D2

Maryland Rd BH16 45 B1
Middlebere Cres BH16 45 B2
Moorings Clo BH15 45 E4
Moriconium Quay BH15 45 C4
Napier Rd BH15 45 A3
Nathan Gdns BH15 45 C3
Normandy Way BH15 45 C3
Norton Way BH15 45 F4
Patchins Rd BH16 45 A2
Peverrell Rd BH16 45 A2
Purbeck Av BH15 45 D4
Redhorn Clo BH16 45 B2
Reuben Dri BH15 45 C3
Rice Gdns BH16 45 C1
Rice Ter BH16 45 C1
Ridgemount Gdns BH15 45 D2
Rigler Rd BH15 45 E4
Rockley Park BH15 45 A2
Rockley Rd BH15 45 D4
Russell Gdns BH16 45 B1
St Michaels Clo BH15 45 D3
Salerno Rd BH15 45 C4
Samson Rd BH15 45 C3
Shapwick Rd BH15 45 F4
Shipstal Clo BH16 45 B1
Solomon Way BH15 45 C3
South Haven Clo BH16 45 A2
Station Rd BH15 45 D3
Symes Rd BH15 45 D1
The Old Rope Walk BH15 45 E4
Tuckers La BH15 45 E4
Turlin Rd BH16 45 A1
Upwey Av BH15 45 D2
Walcheren Pl BH15 45 B2
Winspit Clo BH15 45 D2
Woodlands Av BH15 45 D2
Woodlands Cres BH15 45 D3

LYME REGIS

Anning Rd DT7 33 C4
Applebee Way DT7 33 C3
Avenue Rd DT7 33 C4
Barbers La DT7 33 A2
Bayview Rd DT7 33 C3
Blue Water Dri DT7 33 A4
Bridge St DT7 33 D5
Broad St DT7 33 D4
Charmouth Clo DT7 33 D3
Charmouth Rd DT7 33 D4
Church St, Lyme Regis DT7 33 D4
Church St, Uplyme DT7 33 A2
Clappentail La DT7 33 B4
Clappentail Pk DT7 33 C3
Cobb Rd DT7 33 C5
Colway La DT7 33 C3
Coombe St DT7 33 D4
Coram Av DT7 33 B5
Crogg La DT7 33 A2
Dolphins Clo DT7 33 C4
Dragons Hill DT7 33 D2
East Cliff DT7 33 D4
Elizabeth Clo DT7 33 D3
Fairfield Pk DT7 33 D3
Ferndown Rd DT7 33 D4
Georges Ct DT7 33 D4
Gore La DT7 33 A3
Greenway DT7 33 B4
Hallott Ct DT7 33 C3
Haye Clo DT7 33 B3
Haye La DT7 33 B2
Henrys Way DT7 33 B4
High Cliff Rd DT7 33 B4
Hill Rise Rd DT7 33 C4
Hill Rd DT7 33 C4
Jericho DT7 33 C4
Kings Way DT7 33 C3
Limekiln La DT7 33 A1
Long Entry DT7 33 D4
Lym Clo DT7 33 D4
Lyme Rd DT7 33 A1
Lynch Mill La DT7 33 D4
Manor Av DT7 33 C3
Marine Par DT7 33 C5
Mill Green DT7 33 D4
Mill La DT7 33 B2
Monmouth St DT7 33 D4
North Av DT7 33 C3

Overton Clo DT7 33 D3
Ozone Ter DT7 33 C5
Penny Plot DT7 33 C3
Pine Ridge DT7 33 D3
Pine Walk DT7 33 B5
Pooles Ct DT7 33 D4
Portland Ct DT7 33 B4
Pound La DT7 33 A1
Pound Rd DT7 33 C4
Pound St DT7 33 C4
Prospect Pl DT7 33 C4
Queens Walk DT7 33 C3
Rhode La DT7 33 B1
Roman Rd DT7 33 C4
St Andrews Mdw DT7 33 B3
St Georges Hill DT7 33 B3
St Michaels Gdns DT7 33 C4
Sherborne La DT7 33 C4
Shire La DT7 33 A4
Sidmouth Rd DT7 33 A4
Silver St DT7 33 C4
Somer Fields DT7 33 B3
Somers Rd DT7 33 B4
South Av DT7 33 C3
Spittles La DT7 33 D3
Spring Head Rd DT7 33 A1
Springhill Gdns DT7 33 C3
Staples Ter DT7 33 D4
Stile La DT7 33 C4
Summerhill Rd DT7 33 C3
Talbot Rd DT7 33 C3
Tappers Knap DT7 33 B1
Timber Hill DT7 33 D3
Uplyme Rd DT7 33 B3
Upper Westhill Rd DT7 33 B4
Venlake DT7 33 A2
View Rd DT7 33 A2
Ware La DT7 33 A5
Westhill Rd DT7 33 B4
Whalley La DT7 33 A2
Windsor Ter DT7 33 C3
Woodmead Rd DT7 33 B3
Woodroffe Mdw DT7 33 B3

LYTCHETT MATRAVERS

Abbots Ct BH16 34 C3
Abbotts Mdw BH16 34 C2
Anncott Clo BH16 34 C2
Ballards Clo BH16 34 C2
Blandford Rd Nth BH16 34 F2
Burbidge Clo BH16 34 C4
Castle Farm Rd BH16 34 B2
Charborough Clo BH16 34 B2
Crumplers Clo BH16 34 B2
Deans Drove BH16 34 C3
Dillon Ct BH16 34 C2
Dillons Gdns BH16 34 C4
Eddygreen Rd BH16 34 A4
Eldons Drove BH16 34 B2
Flowers Drove BH16 34 C2
Fosters Spring BH16 34 C3
Foxhills Cres BH16 34 C2
Foxhills Dri BH16 34 C3
Foxhills Rd BH16 34 D2
Friars Ct BH16 34 C2
Frys Ct BH16 34 C2
Gibbs Grn BH16 34 C3
Glebe Rd BH16 34 B4
Hannams Clo BH16 34 B2
High St BH16 34 B1
Hopmans Clo BH16 34 A4
Huntick Est BH16 34 C4
Huntick Rd BH16 34 C2
Jennys La BH16 34 A2
Keates Meadow BH16 34 C3
Landers Reach BH16 34 C3
Lime Kiln Rd BH16 34 D2
Lions Ct BH16 34 D2
Lockyers Way BH16 34 C4
Middle Rd BH16 34 A4
Old Chapel Dri BH16 34 C2
Old Pound Clo BH16 34 B2
Paddock Clo BH16 34 C3
Palmers Orchard BH16 34 C3
Penrose Clo BH16 34 C4
Poole Rd BH16 34 E1
Pryors Walk BH16 34 C3

Prospect Rd BH16 34 C3
Purbeck Clo BH16 34 C2
Purbeck Rd BH16 34 C2
Scutts Clo BH16 34 C2
Spy Clo BH16 34 B2
The Spinney BH16 34 C3
Trenchard Meadow BH16 34 C3
Turbetts Clo BH16 34 B2
Vineyard Clo BH16 34 C2
Wareham Rd BH16 34 B4
Wimborne Rd BH16 34 C2

LYTCHETT MINSTER

Ashbrook Way BH16 35 C2
Dorchester Rd BH16 35 B3
Huntick Rd BH16 35 C1
Lytchett Minster By-Pass BH16 35 B3
New Rd BH16 35 B2
Old Forge Clo BH16 35 C2
Old Watery La BH16 35 C3
Orchard Clo BH16 35 B3
Policemans La BH16 35 D2
Poppy Clo BH16 35 D2
Post Green La BH16 35 B2
Slough La BH16 35 D3

MAIDEN NEWTON

Ashley Av DT2 35 C5
Back La DT2 35 B6
Bull La DT2 35 C5
Cattistock Rd DT2 35 C4
Chapel La DT2 35 C5
Chilfrome La DT2 35 B4
Church Rd DT2 35 C5
Cruxton La DT2 35 C6
Dorchester Rd DT2 35 A5
Drift Rd DT2 35 C4
Frome La DT2 35 C6
Frome Vw DT2 35 D6
Glebe Clo DT2 35 C5
Greenford La DT2 35 B5
Greenford Vw DT2 35 B4
Harvey Clo DT2 35 C5
Hill Vw DT2 35 D6
Newton Rd DT2 35 D6
Norden La DT2 35 C5
North Rd DT2 35 C5
Pound Piece DT2 35 C5
Stanstead Rd DT2 35 C5
Station Rd DT2 35 C5
Webbers Piece DT2 35 C4

POOLE

Adelaide Rd BH15 36 C4
Baiter Gdns BH15 36 C6
Ballard Cl BH15 36 C6
Ballard Rd BH15 36 C6
Balston Ter*, West St BH15 36 B5
Barbers Gate*, Thames St BH15 36 B6
Barbers Piles*, West Quay Rd BH15 36 A5
Barbers Wharf BH15 36 A6
Bay Hog La BH15 36 A5
Bennetts Alley*, Strand St BH15 36 B6
Birds Hill Gdns BH15 36 D4
Birds Hill Rd BH15 36 D3
Blandford Rd BH15 36 A6
Bracken Glen BH15 36 D2
Brailswood Rd BH15 36 D3
Brampton Rd BH15 36 C1
Briar Cl BH15 36 A6
Bridge App BH15 36 A6
Bright Rd BH15 36 D1
Broadstone Way BH15 36 B1
Buffalo Mews*, Market La BH15 36 B5
Canford Rd BH15 36 B5
Carters La BH15 36 B5
Castle St BH15 36 B6

Catalina Dr BH15 36 D6
Chapel La BH15 36 B5
Charles Rd BH15 36 C3
Christopher Cres BH15 36 B1
Church St BH15 36 B6
Churchfield Ct BH15 36 D4
Churchfield Rd BH15 36 D4
Cinnamon La BH15 36 B6
Cobbs La BH15 36 D1
Colborne Cl BH15 36 C5
Connell Rd BH15 36 B2
Corfe Mews BH15 36 D3
Cranes Mews BH15 36 C4
Crow Hill Ct BH15 36 D3
Curlieu Rd BH15 36 D1
Daisy Clo BH15 36 C1
Daniel Gdns*, Skinner St BH15 36 B6
Darbys Cl BH15 36 C1
Darbys La BH15 36 C1
Dear Hay La BH15 36 B5
Dee Way BH15 36 A5
Denby Rd BH15 36 D3
Denmark La BH15 36 C4
Denmark Rd BH15 36 C4
Devon Rd BH15 36 D2
Dingley Rd BH15 36 C1
Dolphin Centre BH15 36 C4
Dorchester Gdns BH15 36 D2
Dorchester Rd BH15 36 C2
Drake Rd BH15 36 B6
East Quay Rd BH15 36 B6
East St BH15 36 B5
Elizabeth Rd BH15 36 C4
Emerson Cl BH15 36 C5
Emerson Rd BH15 36 C5
Enfield Av BH15 36 D1
Enfield Rd BH15 36 D1
Falkland Sq BH15 36 C4
Fernside Rd BH15 36 C2
Ferry Rd BH15 36 B6
Fishermans Rd BH15 36 B6
Fleets Est BH15 36 B1
Fleets La BH15 36 B1
Furnell Rd BH15 36 C6
Gardens Ct BH15 36 D4
Garland Rd BH15 36 C3
Globe La BH15 36 B5
Green Cl BH15 36 C6
Green Gdns BH15 36 C6
Green Rd BH15 36 C5
Guildhall Ct*, New Orchard BH15 36 B5
Harbour Hill Rd BH15 36 D3
Harbour Hl Cres BH15 36 D2
Haynes Av BH15 36 C1
Heath Av BH15 36 C1
Heckford La BH15 36 C3
Heckford Rd BH15 36 C3
Hennings Park Rd BH15 36 C2
High St BH15 36 B6
High St North BH15 36 C4
Hiley Rd BH15 36 C1
Hill St BH15 36 B5
Holes Bay Rd BH15 36 A1
Holly Ct BH15 36 D3
Houlton Rd BH15 36 D3
Hunt Rd BH15 36 D3
Jolliffe Av BH15 36 D3
Jolliffe Rd BH15 36 C3
Kingland Cres BH15 36 C5
Kingland Rd BH15 36 C4
Kings Clo BH15 36 C2
Kingsbere Rd BH15 36 D2
Kingston Rd BH15 36 C3
Kiwi Cl BH15 36 D4
Labrador Dr BH15 36 C6
Lagland St BH15 36 B6
Lander Cl BH15 36 C6
Lansdell Cl BH15 36 D4
Levets La BH15 36 B5
Lions Cl BH15 36 D3
Longfleet Rd BH15 36 C4
Lucas Rd BH15 36 B6
Manor Pk BH15 36 B2
Maple Rd BH15 36 C4
Market Cl BH15 36 B5
Market St BH15 36 B5
Marlott Rd BH15 36 C2
Marnhull Rd BH15 36 D1
Marston Rd BH15 36 B5
Mellstock Rd BH15 36 D1
Middle St BH15 36 D1
Milestone Rd BH15 36 C1

Mount Pleasant Rd BH15 36 C4
Nansen Av BH15 36 C2
New Harbour Rd BH15 36 B6
New Harbour Rd West BH15 36 A6
New Orchard BH15 36 B5
New Quay Rd BH15 36 A6
New St BH15 36 B5
Newfoundland Dr BH15 36 C5
North St BH15 36 B5
Norton Way BH15 36 A6
Oakdale Rd BH15 36 D1
Oakfield Rd BH15 36 C1
Old Orchard BH15 36 B5
Old Town Mews*, Market Cl BH15 36 B5
Palmer Rd BH15 36 B2
Paradise St BH15 36 B6
Parish Rd BH15 36 D4
Park Lake Rd BH15 36 D5
Parkstone Rd BH15 36 C4
Perry Gdns BH15 36 C5
Pitwines Cl BH15 36 C5
Popes Rd BH15 36 C1
Poplar Cl*, West St BH15 36 B5
Pound La BH15 36 D2
Preston Rd BH15 36 B1
Prosperous St BH15 36 B5
Rectory Rd BH15 36 B1
Rodney Ct*, Whatleigh Cl BH15 36 C5
Rose Ct BH15 36 D4
Rowland Av BH15 36 D2
Saint Aubyns Ct BH15 36 B5
Saint Clements La BH15 36 A6
Saint James Cl BH15 36 B5
Saint Johns Rd BH15 36 C3
Saint Margarets Rd BH15 36 C3
Saint Marys Rd BH15 36 C3
Sandbourne Rd BH15 36 C3
Sandpit La BH15 36 D4
Sarum St BH15 36 B6
School La BH15 36 B2
Seldown BH15 36 C4
Seldown Bridge BH15 36 C5
Seldown La BH15 36 C4
Seldown Rd BH15 36 D4
Seliot Cl BH15 36 D2
Serpentine La Sth BH15 36 C4
Serpentine Rd BH15 36 C4
Shaftesbury Rd BH15 36 C4
Sherrin Cl BH15 36 C2
Shottsford Rd BH15 36 C2
Simmonds Cl BH15 36 C2
Skinner St BH15 36 B6
Slip Way BH15 36 B5
Somerby Rd BH15 36 D1
South Rd BH15 36 C5
Sovereign Business Pk BH15 36 B1
Stadium Way BH15 36 C4
Stanley Ct BH15 36 C1
Stanley Green Cres BH15 36 B2
Stanley Grn Ind Est BH15 36 B2
Stanley Green Rd BH15 36 B2
Stanley Rd BH 15 36 C6
Station Rd BH15 36 A6
Stenhurst Rd BH15 36 D1
Sterte Av BH15 36 B3
Sterte Av West BH15 36 B3
Sterte Cl BH15 36 B3
Sterte Esp BH15 36 B3
Sterte Ind Est BH15 36 B3
Sterte Rd BH15 36 B3
Stokes Av BH15 36 C3
Strand St BH15 36 B6
Tatnam Cres BH15 36 C3
Tatnam La BH15 36 C3
Tatnam Rd BH15 36 B3
Taverner Cl BH15 36 D5
Thames Mews BH15 36 B6
Thames St BH15 36 B6
The Quay BH15 36 A6
Towngate Bridge BH15 36 B5

Towngate Shopping Centre BH15 36 B5
Vallis Cl BH15 36 C6
Vicarage Rd BH15 36 B1
Waldren Cl BH15 36 D5
Walking Field La BH15 36 C5
Waverley Cres BH15 36 C1
Well La BH15 36 C3
Wessex Gate Retail Pk BH15 36 A1
West Butts St BH15 36 B5
West Quay Rd BH15 36 A5
West St BH15 36 B5
West View Rd BH15 36 B3
Westons La BH15 36 B5
Whatleigh Cl BH15 36 C5
White Horse Dr BH15 36 B2
Whittles Way BH15 36 A5
Wilkins Way BH15 36 A5
Willis Way BH15 36 B1
Wilmur Cres BH15 36 D1
Wimborne Rd BH15 36 C1
Wingfield Av BH15 36 D1
Winifred Rd BH15 36 D2
Winterbourne Cl BH15 36 C2
Winterbourne Rd BH15 36 C2

PRESTON

Allberry Gdns DT3 37 A3
Barton Dri DT3 37 B3
Baydon Clo DT3 37 B3
Bridge Inn La DT3 37 C2
Brookmead Clo DT3 37 C1
Brookside Clo DT3 37 C3
Brunel Dri DT3 37 B2
Cedar Dri DT3 37 B3
Chalbury Clo DT3 37 A3
Chalbury Lodge DT3 37 B3
Church Rd DT3 37 C3
Churchward Av DT3 37 B2
Collet Clo DT3 37 C1
Coombe Valley Rd DT3 37 A1
Cornhill Way DT3 37 C1
Emminster Clo DT3 37 A3
Fir Dri DT3 37 C2
Fisherbridge Rd DT3 37 C3
Forehill Clo DT3 37 B3
Halstock Clo DT3 37 A3
Hambro Ter DT3 37 C3
Hawksworth Clo DT3 37 B2
Hazel Dri DT3 37 B3
Holcombe Clo DT3 37 C3
Horyford Clo DT3 37 C3
Littlemoor Rd DT3 37 A3
Marley Clo DT3 37 C2
Maunsell Av DT3 37 B2
Mawdywalls DT3 37 C2
Medway Dri DT3 37 A3
Mill La DT3 37 C2
Millers Clo DT3 37 C2
Mission Hall La DT3 37 C1
Moorcombe Dri DT3 37 B2
Old Bincombe La DT3 37 C3
Old Granary Clo DT3 37 C2
Osmington Hill DT3 37 D2
Plaisters La DT3 37 C1
Preston Rd DT3 37 B3
Puddledock La DT3 37 C2
Reynards Way DT3 37 C2
Rhosewood Dri DT3 37 C2
Rimbrow Clo DT3 37 C2
Rymbury DT3 37 C2
Seven Acres Rd DT3 37 C1
Silver St DT3 37 C1
Stanier Rd DT3 37 C2
Stroudley Cres DT3 37 B3
Sunnyfields DT3 37 C2
Sutton Clo DT3 37 C1
Sutton Court Lawns DT3 37 C1
Sutton Pk DT3 37 D2
Sutton Rd DT3 37 C2
Tallidge Clo DT3 37 C3
Telford Clo DT3 37 C2
The Weir DT3 37 C2
Valley Clo DT3 37 C2
Verlands Rd DT3 37 C2
Wainwright Clo DT3 37 C2
White Horse Dri DT3 37 C1
White Horse La DT3 37 C1
Willow Cres DT3 37 B3

Winslow Rd DT3 37 C2

PUDDLETOWN

Ash Tree Clo DT2 37 B6
Athelhampton Rd DT2 37 B6
Back St DT2 37 B5
Backwater DT2 37 B5
Beech Rd DT2 37 B6
Bellbury Clo DT2 37 B6
Blandford Rd DT2 37 A5
Brymer Rd DT2 37 B6
Butt Clo DT2 37 B6
Chapel Vw DT2 37 B6
Charminster La DT2 37 A5
Cobbs Pl DT2 37 B6
Coombe Rd DT2 37 B6
Doctors La DT2 37 B5
Dorchester Rd DT2 37 A6
Druce La DT2 37 A4
Greenacres DT2 37 A5
High St DT2 37 A5
Kingsmead DT2 37 A6
Long La DT2 37 B4
Mill St DT2 37 B5
Millom La DT2 37 B6
New St DT2 37 B6
Orford St DT2 37 B5
Rod Hill La DT2 37 B6
Styles La DT2 37 B6
The Coombe DT2 37 A6
The Green DT2 37 B6
The Square DT2 37 B5
Thompson Clo DT2 37 A4
Three Lanes Way DT2 37 A5
Walpole St DT2 37 B5
Whitehill DT2 37 B6
Willoughby Clo DT2 37 B6

SHAFTESBURY

Abbey Clo SP7 38 C3
Abbey Walk SP7 38 C3
Angel La SP7 38 C2
Ash Clo SP7 38 D1
Barton Clo SP7 38 C2
Barton Hill SP7 38 C2
Beaufoy Clo SP7 38 E2
Bell St SP7 38 C2
Belmont Clo SP7 38 D3
Bimport SP7 38 B3
Blackmore Rd SP7 38 E1
Bleke St SP7 38 C2
Boundary Rd SP7 38 D3
Boyne Mead SP7 38 D3
Boyne Mead Clo SP7 38 D3
Breach La SP7 38 B3
Brinscombe La SP7 38 D4
Brionne Way SP7 38 E2
Burton Clo SP7 38 E2
Butts Mead SP7 38 D4
Calves La SP7 38 A1
Castle Hill Clo SP7 38 B2
Charles Garrett Clo*, Coppice St SP7 38 D2
Christys Gdns SP7 38 D2
Church Hill SP7 38 A2
Church Walk SP7 38 C3
Coppice St SP7 38 D2
Cranbourne Dri SP7 38 D1
Crookhays SP7 38 D1
Dark La SP7 38 C2
Deansleigh Pk SP7 38 E2
Downlands SP7 38 E2
Fairlane SP7 38 E3
Fountains Mead SP7 38 D1
Foyle Hill SP7 38 A4
French Mill Rise SP7 38 D3
Frenchmill La SP7 38 D2
Gillingham Rd SP7 38 A1
Gold Hill SP7 38 C3
Gower Rd SP7 38 E2
Granville Gdns SP7 38 D2
Great Grounds SP7 38 E1
Great La SP7 38 D3
Grosvenor Rd SP7 38 D1
Haimes La SP7 38 C2
Hawkesdene SP7 38 D3
Hawkesdene La SP7 38 D3
Hawthorne Clo SP7 38 E1

Heathfields Way SP7	38 D1	Well La SP7	38 B2	Marston Rd DT9	39 A1	Hine Town La DT11	40 B5	Woodmill Clo DT10 41 C1
High St SP7	38 C3	Westminster Clo SP7	38 B2	McCreery Rd DT9	39 D1	Holloway La DT11	40 C6	
Higher Blandford Rd SP7	38 E4	Whitehart La SP7	38 C3	Midleaze DT9	39 A3	Homefield DT11	40 C2	

STURMINSTER NEWTON

Homefield SP7	38 D1	Win Green Vw SP7	38 E2	Mulberry Gdns DT9	39 C1	Honeysuckle Gdns DT11	40 B6	Alder Clo DT10	41 D5
Horse Ponds SP7	38 B2	Wincombe La SP7	38 D2	Nethercoombe La DT9	39 B1	Jacobs Ladder DT11	40 C2	Alder Rd DT10	41 D4
Imber Rd SP7	38 E2	Windmill Clo SP7	38 D1	New Rd DT9	39 D4	Knapps DT11	40 A4	Badgers Way DT10	41 C4
Jeaneau Clo SP7	38 D2	Woodman Ct*,		Newell DT9	39 C2	Knotts Clo DT11	40 C2	Barnes Clo DT10	41 B5
Jubilee Path SP7	38 C3	Coppice St SP7	38 D3	Newland DT9	39 D2	Lanchards DT11	40 A5	Bath Rd DT10	41 B5
Jude Ct*, Bimport SP7	38 C3	Woolands La SP7	38 B2	Newland Dri DT9	39 E2	Lanchards La DT11	40 A6	Bridge St DT10	41 A6
King Alfreds Way SP7	38 D2	Yeatmans Clo SP7	38 B2	Noake Rd DT9	39 B4	Little La DT11	40 A4	Brinsley Clo DT10	41 A4
Kings Hill SP7	38 C2	Yeatmans La SP7	38 B2	North Rd DT9	39 D2	Melway Gdns DT11	40 D3	Brinsley Ct DT10	41 A4
Kingsbere La SP7	38 E2			Oborne Rd DT9	39 E2	Melway La DT11	40 C3	Brinsley Mead DT10	41 A4
Kingsman La SP7	38 C3	**SHERBORNE**		Old Farm East & West		Millbrook Clo DT11	40 C1	Buffets Clo DT10	41 B4
Laneside SP7	38 D1			DT9	39 C2	Netmead La DT11	40 B1	Buffets Rd DT10	41 B4
Langfords La SP7	38 B3			Ottery La DT9	39 C4	Nutmead Clo DT11	40 C1	Butts Pond DT10	41 C5
Laundry La SP7	38 B3	Abbey Clo DT9	39 D3	Pageant Dri DT9	39 D3	Olivers Mead DT11	40 C1	Church La DT10	41 B5
Layton La SP7	38 C3	Abbey Rd DT9	39 D3	Pinford La DT9	39 F2	Pepper Hill DT11	40 B6	Church St DT10	41 B5
Linden Park SP7	38 E3	Abbots Way DT9	39 A4	Powys La DT9	39 C3	Poplar Hill DT11	40 A5	Church Walk DT10	41 B6
Lindlar Clo SP7	38 D2	Acreman Ct DT9	39 C2	Priestlands DT9	39 D3	Portman Dri DT11	40 C1	Coles Clo DT10	41 C5
Little Content La SP7	38 D2	Acreman Pl DT9	39 D3	Priestlands La DT9	39 D2	Puxey La DT11	40 A6	Denhall Clo DT10	41 B4
Little Down SP7	38 D1	Acreman St DT9	39 C2	Quarr Dr DT9	39 D1	Rectory La DT11	40 C2	Durrant DT10	41 A5
Long Cross SP7	38 A2	Admiral Way DT9	39 E1	Quarr La DT9	39 D1	Ridgeway La DT11	40 C1	Elm Clo DT10	41 C5
Long Mead SP7	38 D2	Albany Clo DT9	39 E1	Raleigh Ct DT9	39 E3	St Nicholas Ct DT11	40 D2	Filbridge Rise DT10	41 C4
Love La SP7	38 B3	Askwith Clo DT9	39 A4	Richmond Clo DT9	39 C3	**St Patricks Ind Est**		Friars Moor DT10	41 C5
Lower Blandford Rd		Back La DT9	39 D2	Richmond Grn DT9	39 C3	DT11	40 B4	Gotts Corner DT10	41 B6
SP7	38 D3	Barton Gdns DT9	39 B2	Richmond Rd DT9	39 C3	Sandy La DT11	40 D1	Gotts La DT10	41 B6
Lyons Walk SP7	38 C3	Bede St DT9	39 E2	Ridgeway DT9	39 B4	Schelin Way DT11	40 B6	Goughs Clo DT10	41 B5
Magdalane La SP7	38 C3	Blackberry La DT9	39 C2	St Catherines Cres		Seymer Clo DT11	40 A4	Green Clo DT10	41 D5
Mampitts La SP7	38 E3	Bradford Rd DT9	39 A3	DT9	39 B3	Shaftesbury Rd DT11	40 C1	Hambledon View DT10	41 D5
Mampitts Rd SP7	38 E3	Bridewell Ct DT9	39 D3	St Catherines Way		Shepherds La DT11	40 C2	Hanover Clo DT10	41 C4
Maple Clo SP7	38 D1	Bristol Rd DT9	39 D1	DT9	39 B3	Shillingstone La DT11	40 A5	Hinton View DT10	41 C4
Meadow Clo SP7	38 D1	Castle Rd DT9	39 E1	St Marys Rd DT9	39 B3	Southfield La DT11	40 B3	Lane-Fox Ter DT10	41 C5
Melbury Way SP7	38 E2	Castle Town Way DT9	39 E1	St Pauls Clo DT9	39 E1	Spencer Gdns DT11	40 C6	Manston Rd DT10	41 C4
Motcombe Rd SP7	38 C1	Castleton DT9	39 E2	St Pauls Grn DT9	39 E1	Stansway Ct DT11	40 A4	Market Cross DT10	41 B5
Mustons La SP7	38 C2	Castleton Rd DT9	39 E2	St Swithins Clo DT9	39 E2	Station Rd,		Market Pl DT10	41 B5
Nettlebed Nursery SP7	38 B2	Chandlers DT9	39 E1	St Swithins Rd DT9	39 E2	Child Okeford DT11	40 C3	Penny St DT10	41 B5
Nettlecombe SP7	38 E2	Cheap St DT9	39 D2	School Dri DT9	39 E2	Station Rd,		Pitts Orchard DT10	41 B4
New La SP7	38 F4	Chrysanthemum Row		School La DT9	39 D3	Shillingstone DT11	40 A4	Quarry Clo DT10	41 C4
New Rd SP7	38 B2	DT9	39 D3	Sheeplands La DT9	39 B2	Stour Clo DT11	40 C6	Rabin Hill DT10	41 C4
Old St SP7	38 D3	Church Pl DT9	39 D3	Simons Rd DT9	39 D1	The Butts DT11	40 D3	Ricketts La DT10	41 A5
Oxencroft SP7	38 D1	Clanfield DT9	39 A4	South Av DT9	39 B4	The Cross,		Rivers Mead DT10	41 C4
Paddock Clo SP7	38 E4	Coldharbour DT9	39 D2	South Ct DT9	39 B4	Child Okeford DT11	40 C2	Rixon Clo DT10	41 C5
Park La SP7	38 C3	Cooks La DT9	39 D3	South St DT9	39 D3	The Cross,		Shortedge DT10	41 B5
Park Walk SP7	38 C3	Coombe Rd DT9	39 B1	Springfield Cres DT9	39 C3	Shillingstone DT11	40 A5	Station Rd DT10	41 B5
Parsons Pool SP7	38 C2	Cornhill DT9	39 C2	Station Rd DT9	39 D3	The Hollow DT11	40 C1	The Row DT10	41 B5
Pine Walk SP7	38 B3	Culvers Clo DT9	39 C3	Stonedene DT9	39 D1	Upper Street DT11	40 D2	West End DT10	41 B5
Pix Mead Gdns SP7	38 E3	Digby Rd DT9	39 D3	Swan Yard DT9	39 D2	Wessex Av DT11	40 B6	White Lane Clo DT10	41 B4
Pound La SP7	38 D3	Dorchester Rd DT9	39 C4	The Avenue DT9	39 E2				
Raspberry La SP7	38 B3	Dunston St DT9	39 E2	The Furlongs DT9	39 D1	**STALBRIDGE**		**SWANAGE/ LANGTON MATRAVERS**	
Ratcliffs Gdns SP7	38 B2	Durrant Pl DT9	39 D3	The Green DT9	39 D3				
Ridgeway SP7	38 D1	Earls Clo DT9	39 E1	The Hayes DT9	39 D3				
Rowan Clo SP7	38 E1	East Mill La DT9	39 E3	The Maltings DT9	39 E3	Barrow Hill DT10	41 A3		
Rumbolds Rd SP7	38 D3	Finger La DT9	39 D3	The Sheeplands DT9	39 B1	Bibberne Row DT10	41 C3	Aigburth Rd BH19	43 E3
Rutter Clo SP7	38 D3	Fosters DT9	39 E2	The Wilderness DT9	39 E2	Blackmore Rd DT10	41 C2	Alderbury Clo BH19	42 D4
St Edwards Clo SP7	38 D2	Gainsborough Dri DT9	39 A3	Thornbank Ct DT9	39 E3	Boyle Clo DT10	41 C2	Ancaster Rd BH19	43 E3
St Georges Rd SP7	38 D3	Gainsborough Hill		Tinneys La DT9	39 E2	Cale Clo DT10	41 D3	Anglebury Av BH19	43 F2
St James St SP7	38 B3	DT9	39 E4	Trendle St DT9	39 D3	Church Hill DT10	41 B1	Anvil Clo BH19	42 D4
St Jamess Common		Gas House La DT9	39 E3	Trent Path La DT9	39 A1	Church Walk DT10	41 A1	Argyle Rd BH19	43 F4
SP7	38 B4	George St DT9	39 D2	Underdown La DT9	39 F1	Coppern Way DT10	41 C3	Ash Clo BH19	42 D4
St Johns Hill SP7	38 B3	Granville Way DT9	39 E1	Vernalls Rd DT9	39 D1	Drews La DT10	41 B1	Atlantic Rd BH19	43 F5
St Lawrences Cres SP7	38 D1	Gravel Pits DT9	39 D3	West Mill La DT9	39 C4	Duck La DT10	41 B1	Ballard Est BH19	43 G1
St Martins La SP7	38 D3	Greenhill DT9	39 D2	Westbridge Pk DT9	39 B4	Duncliffe Clo DT10	41 D2	Ballard Lee BH19	43 G1
Salisbury Rd SP7	38 D3	Half Acres DT9	39 C3	Westbury DT9	39 C4	Gold St DT10	41 B2	Ballard Rd BH19	43 G1
Salisbury St SP7	38 D3	Half Moon La DT9	39 D3	Westfield DT9	39 B4	Grosvenor Rd DT10	41 B3	Ballard Way BH19	43 G1
Sally Kings La SP7	38 B2	Half Moon St DT9	39 D3	Widforth Clo DT9	39 A4	Grove La DT10	41 B2	Battlegate Footway	
Savoy Ct*,		Harbour Rd DT9	39 E1	Wingfield Rd DT9	39 C3	Grove La Clo DT10	41 B2	BH19	43 G3
Bimport SP7	38 C3	Harbour Way DT9	39 D1	Wootton Gro DT9	39 D1	Hardy Cres DT10	41 C2	Battlemead BH19	43 F2
Saxon Spur SP7	38 D2	Hardings House La		Wynnes Clo DT9	39 B3	High St DT10	41 B1	Bay Clo BH19	43 G1
Shaftesbury By-Pass		DT9	39 A1	Wynnes Rise DT9	39 D1	Jarvis Clo DT10	41 C3	Bay Cres BH19	43 G1
SP7	38 B2	Higher Cheap St DT9	39 D2	Yeovil Rd DT9	39 A3	Jarvis Way DT10	41 C2	Beach Gdns BH19	43 F3
Shiphouse La SP7	38 C4	Highmore Rd DT9	39 B1			Larks Mdw DT10	41 C3	Bell St BH19	42 D4
Shooters La SP7	38 C3	Hill Brow DT9	39 B4	**SHILLINGSTONE CHILD OKEFORD**		Lower Rd DT10	41 C3	Belle Vue Rd BH19	43 G5
Shooters Paddock SP7	38 C3	Hill House Clo DT9	39 E2			Meadow Clo DT10	41 C2	Belvedere Rd BH19	43 G5
Snakey La SP7	38 C3	Honeycombe Rise DT9	39 B4			New Rd DT10	41 C2	Benleaze Way BH19	42 D4
Spring Field SP7	38 D1	Horsecastles DT9	39 C3			Park Gro DT10	41 A2	Bon Accord Rd BH19	43 F5
Stoney Path SP7	38 B3	Horsecastles La DT9	39 B3	Allen Clo DT11	40 C3	Park Rd DT10	41 A2	Bonfields Av BH19	43 F2
Sturminster Rd SP7	38 B4	Hospital La DT9	39 D2	Aplands Clo DT11	40 B1	Pond Walk DT10	41 B2	Boundary Clo BH19	43 G6
Sweetmans Rd SP7	38 D2	Hound St DT9	39 D3	Apple Acre DT11	40 C1	Raleigh Rd DT10	41 C3	Brickyard La BH19	43 E1
Tanyard La SP7	38 B3	Hunts Mead DT9	39 A4	Bere Marsh DT11	40 A3	Ring St DT10	41 C3	Broad Rd BH19	43 G4
Ten Acres SP7	38 E2	Kings Cres DT9	39 D1	Blandford Rd DT11	40 B5	Robinson Heights		Burlington Rd BH19	43 G2
The Beeches SP7	38 B4	Kings Rd DT9	39 C2	Brodham Way DT11	40 A6	DT10	41 C2	Burnhams La BH19	42 C2
The Butts SP7	38 A2	Kitt Hill DT9	39 C2	Candys La DT11	40 B5	Silk House Barton		Burts Pl*,	
The Commons SP7	38 B2	Knotts Paddock DT9	39 E2	Chalwell DT11	40 C3	DT10	41 B2	BH19	43 G4
The Knapp SP7	38 B2	Lambsfield DT9	39 E1	Church Rd DT11	40 B5	Springfields DT10	41 D3	Casterbridge Clo BH19	42 D4
The Venn SP7	38 B2	Langdons DT9	39 E1	Cookswell DT11	40 A4	Stalbridge Clo DT10	41 D3	Cauldron Av BH19	43 F3
Thomas Hardy Dri SP7	38 E2	Left Ct DT9	39 B4	Coombe La DT11	40 B6	Station Rd DT10	41 B2	Cauldron Barn Rd	
Tobys Ct SP7	38 C2	Lenthay Clo DT9	39 B4	Duck St DT11	40 D3	Sturminster Rd DT10	41 D3	BH19	43 F2
Tollgate Park SP7	38 D1	Lenthay Rd DT9	39 B4	Everetts La DT11	40 B6	The Hawthorns DT10	41 D3	Cauldron Cres BH19	43 F2
Tout Hill SP7	38 B2	Littlefield DT9	39 B4	Gold Hill DT11	40 B1	The Paddocks DT10	41 D3	Cauldron Mdws BH19	43 F2
Umbers Hill SP7	38 B3	Long St DT9	39 D3	Greenway DT11	40 C2	Thrift Clo DT10	41 C3		
Vale Vw*,		Lower Acreman St		Greenway La DT11	40 B2	Vale Rd DT10	41 C2		
Bimport SP7	38 C3	DT9	39 D3	Gunn La DT11	40 B6	Waterlake DT10	41 C3		
Victoria St SP7	38 C2	Ludbourne Rd DT9	39 E3	Hayward La DT11	40 C2	Wessex Rd DT10	41 D3		
Watery La SP7	38 C3	Manor Ct DT9	39 D2	High St DT11	40 C2	Wood La DT10	41 A3		

Cecil Rd BH19 43 E4
Chapel La BH19 43 F4
Church Clo BH19 43 F4
Church Hill BH19 43 F4
Cliff Av BH19 43 G2
Clifton Clo BH19 43 G2
Clifton Rd BH19 43 G2
Cluny Cres BH19 43 G4
Commercial Rd BH19 43 G4
Coombe Hill BH19 42 B4
Cornwall Rd BH19 43 F4
Court Hill BH19 43 F4
Court Rd BH19 43 F4
Cow La BH19 43 E4
Cowlease BH19 43 F4
Crack La BH19 42 A3
Cranborne Rd BH19 43 F4
D'Urberville Dri BH19 43 F2
Darkie La BH19 43 E1
Days Rd BH19 42 D4
De Moulham Rd BH19 43 G2
Dolphin Clo BH19 43 F3
Drummond Rd BH19 43 G5
Durlston Farm BH19 43 F1
Durlston Rd BH19 43 G4
Durnford Drove BH19 42 A5
Durnford Pl BH19 43 G4
East Gro BH19 42 A4
Eldon Ter BH19 43 F4
Encombe Rd BH19 43 G4
Exeter Rd BH19 43 G4
Findlay Pl BH19 43 E4
Foxhill La BH19 43 E4
Gannetts Pk BH19 43 F3
Gilbert Rd BH19 43 F4
Globe Clo BH19 43 G2
Godlington La BH19 42 D2
Gordon Rd BH19 43 F4
Grosvenor Rd BH19 43 G5
Gypshayes BH19 42 A4
Hanbury Rd BH19 43 E4
Heather Clo BH19 43 E4
Hendrie Clo BH19 43 E4
High Cliff Rd BH19 43 G2
High St, Langton
  Matravers BH19 42 A4
High St,
  Swanage BH19 42 D4
Hill Rd BH19 43 F1
Hillsea Rd BH19 43 E4
Hillview Rd BH19 43 E4
Hoborne Rd BH19 43 E4
Holmes Rd BH19 42 C4
Howard Rd BH19 43 E4
Ilminster Rd BH19 43 F3
Institute Rd BH19 43 G4
James Day Mead BH19 43 F1
Jubilee Rd BH19 42 D4
King Edwards Av BH19 43 F2
Kings Rd East BH19 43 G4
Kings Rd West BH19 43 F4
Kingswood Clo BH19 42 D4
Knollsea Clo BH19 43 G5
Leeson Clo BH19 42 D4
Lighthouse Rd BH19 43 G6
Linden Rd BH19 43 E4
Locarno Rd BH19 43 F4
Lower Steppes BH19 42 B4
Manor Rd BH19 43 G4
Manwell Dri BH19 43 F5
Manwell Rd BH19 43 F5
Manwells La*,
  High St BH19 43 E4
Mariners Dri BH19 43 E4
Marsh Way BH19 42 D4
Marshall Row BH19 43 G4
Mermaid Pl*,
  Station Pl BH19 43 G4
Moor Rd BH19 43 F1
Morrison Rd BH19 43 G4
Mount Pleasant BH19 42 A4
Mount Pleasant La
  BH19 43 G4
Mount Scars BH19 43 F5
Newton Manor Clo
  BH19 43 E4
Newton Manor Gdns
  BH19 43 E4
Newton Rise BH19 43 E4
Newton Rd BH19 43 G5
North St BH19 42 A4
Northbrook Rd BH19 43 F1
Old Malthouse Rd
  BH19 42 A4
Osborne Rd BH19 43 F4
Ismay Rd BH19 43 G6

Panorama Rd BH19 43 E4
Park Rd BH19 43 G4
Peveril Heights*,
  Marshal Row BH19 43 G4
Peveril Point Rd BH19 43 H4
Peveril Rd BH19 43 G5
Plantation Clo BH19 43 E5
Priests Rd BH19 43 E4
Priests Way BH19 42 C5
Princess Rd BH19 43 F4
Prospect Cres BH19 43 E3
Purbeck Ter BH19 43 G5
Purbeck Vw BH19 43 E4
Quarry Clo BH19 43 E4
Queens Mead BH19 43 F4
Queens Rd BH19 43 F4
Rabling Rd BH19 43 F3
Redcliff Rd BH19 43 G1
Rempstone Back Rd
  BH19 43 G3
Rempstone Rd BH19 43 G3
Richmond Rd BH19 43 F4
Rough Heights BH19 43 F5
Russell Av BH19 43 F5
Russell Dri BH19 43 F5
St Georges Clo BH19 42 A4
St Vast Rd BH19 43 G5
Salisbury Rd BH19 43 G5
Sambourne Clo BH19 42 D4
Seaward Rd BH19 43 G2
Sentry Rd BH19 43 G4
Serrells Mead BH19 42 B4
Seymer Rd BH19 43 G4
Shaston Clo BH19 42 D4
Shirley Clo BH19 43 E4
Shore Rd BH19 43 G2
Shottsford Clo BH19 42 D4
Solent Rd BH19 43 G6
South Cliff Rd BH19 43 G6
South Rd BH19 43 E4
Springfield Rd BH19 43 F4
Stafford Rd BH19 43 G4
Station Pl BH19 43 G4
Station Rd BH19 43 G4
Steer Rd BH19 43 E4
Steppes BH19 42 B4
Steppes Hill BH19 42 B4
Streche Rd BH19 43 G1
Sunnydale Rd BH19 43 G5
Sunridge Clo BH19 43 G5
Sunshine Walk BH19 43 F4
Sydenham Rd BH19 42 C4
Taunton Rd BH19 43 G4
The Hyde BH19 42 A4
The Parade BH19 43 G4
Three Acre La BH19 42 B4
Toms Field BH19 42 A4
Town Hall La*,
  Kings Rd East BH19 43 G4
Townsend Rd BH19 43 F4
Ulwell Rd BH19 43 F1
Valley Rd BH19 42 B3
Victoria Av BH19 43 G3
Victoria Rd BH19 43 G2
Victoria Ter*,
  Jubilee Rd BH19 42 D4
Vivian Pk BH19 43 F2
Walrond Rd BH19 43 F3
Washpond La, Langton
  Matravers BH19 42 D2
Washpond La,
  New Swanage BH19 43 E1
Wessex Ct*, De
  Moulham La BH19 43 G2
Wessex Way BH19 43 F2
West Dri BH19 43 E4
West Durlston La BH19 43 G5
Whitecliff Rd BH19 43 F1
Wills Rd BH19 43 E4
Wilson Ct*,
  Durnford Pl BH19 43 G4
York Ter BH19 43 G4

UPTON

Allens La BH16 44 E4
Allens Rd BH16 44 D3
Arne View Clo BH16 44 C2
Ash Clo BH16 44 C2
Ballam Clo BH16 44 D2
Barn Clo BH16 44 B3
Bay Clo BH16 44 C4
Beach Rd BH16 44 B3

Beacon Park Cres
  BH16 44 B2
Beacon Park Rd BH16 44 B2
Beacon Rd BH16 44 C2
Beechbank Av BH17 44 F1
Bell Heather Clo BH16 44 C2
Birchwood Rd BH16 44 C3
Blackbird Clo BH17 44 F1
Blandford Rd BH16 44 D3
Blandford Rd Nth BH16 44 B1
Blandford Rd Nth BH16 44 C2
Border Dri BH16 44 D4
Border Rd BH16 44 D4
Briarswood Rd BH16 44 D2
Bridle Clo BH16 44 E3
Cedar Clo BH16 44 C2
Chelmsford Rd BH16 44 C3
Cherry Hill Gro BH16 44 C3
Chris Cres BH16 44 D2
Coronation Av BH16 44 C2
Dacombe Clo BH16 44 D2
Dacombe Dri BH16 44 D2
Darrian Ct BH16 44 C2
Davenport Clo BH16 44 D2
Dorchester Rd BH16 44 A2
Douglas Clo BH16 44 C2
Douglas Mews BH16 44 C2
Doussie Clo BH16 44 B2
Egdon Ct BH16 44 C2
Elizabeth Rd BH15 44 D2
Factory Rd BH16 44 D3
Firsway BH16 44 D2
Foxgloves BH16 44 C2
Franklyn Clo BH16 44 C2
Frenchs Farm Rd BH16 44 B2
Furzey Rd BH16 44 C3
Goldfinch Rd BH17 44 F1
Gorse La BH16 44 D2
Grebe Clo BH17 44 F2
Greenacre Clo BH16 44 D3
Greenway Cres BH16 44 B3
Guest Rd BH16 44 C2
Gurjun Clo BH16 44 B2
Gwenlyn Rd BH16 44 D3
Heatherbrae La BH16 44 C4
Heatherdell BH16 44 B3
Heights Rd BH16 44 D2
Hibbs Clo BH16 44 D2
Hickory Clo BH16 44 B2
Holcombe Rd BH16 44 C3
Holly Clo BH16 44 B2
Hop Clo BH16 44 A3
Huntick Rd BH16 44 A2
Kestrel Clo BH16 44 C2
Larch Clo BH17 44 F1
Llewellin Clo BH16 44 D2
Llewellin Ct BH16 44 D2
Longmeadow La BH17 44 F2
Lytchett Way BH16 44 C3
Marsh La BH16 44 B2
Martingale Clo BH16 44 E2
Meadow Bank BH16 44 D2
Meadows Clo BH16 44 D2
Meadows Dri BH16
  BH17 44 D2
Meadowsweet Rd BH17 44 F1
Minster Way BH16 44 C2
Moorland Cres BH16 44 C3
Moorland Par BH16 44 C2
Moorland Way BH16 44 C3
Oak Rd BH16 44 D3
Oakley Gdns BH16 44 B2
Oasis Mews BH16 44 B2
Old Bound Rd BH16 44 D4
Old Kiln Rd BH16 44 E3
Otter Clo BH16 44 C3
Palmerston Clo BH16 44 D2
Palmerston Rd BH16 44 D2
Pearce Rd BH16 44 C3
Peters Clo BH16 44 D3
Pine View Clo BH16 44 D3
Pinewood Clo BH16 44 B2
Pinewood Rd BH16 44 B2
Policemans La BH16 44 A3
Pony Dri BH16 44 E2
Poole Rd BH16 44 D3
Poppy Clo BH16 44 A2
Preston Clo BH16 44 D3
Purbeck Clo BH16 44 C3
Randalls Hill BH16 44 A1
Redwood Rd BH16 44 C2
Richard Clo BH16 44 C2
Ropers La BH16 44 E3
St Annes Rd BH16 44 C2
St Davids Rd BH16 44 C2
St Martins Rd BH16 44 B2

Saltings Rd BH16 44 C3
Sandy La BH16 44 B3
Sea View Rd BH16 44 B3
Seabank Clo BH16 44 B3
Shirley Rd BH16 44 C2
Shore Av BH16 44 D4
Shore Clo BH16 44 D4
Shore Gdns BH16 44 C4
Shore La BH16 44 C4
Slough La BH16 44 A3
Stirrup Clo BH16 44 E2
Stuart Clo BH16 44 D2
The Crossways BH16 44 D3
The Triangle BH16 44 C2
The Ventura Centre
  BH16 44 E3
Tree Hamlets BH16 44 D4
Turbary Ct BH16 44 D2
Upton By-Pass BH16 44 A2
Upton Clo BH16 44 C2
Upton Ct BH16 44 C2
Upton Heath Est BH16 44 D2
Ventura Pl BH16 44 E3
Warbler Clo BH16 44 C2
Watery La BH16 44 A3
Willow Clo BH16 44 E4
Woodcote Dri BH16 44 C3
Woodpecker Dri BH17 44 F2
Yarrells Clo BH16 44 D3
Yarrells Dri BH16 44 C3
Yarrells La BH16 44 D3

UPWEY/BROADWEY

Alamanda Rd DT3 46 D6
Bayard Rd DT3 46 C6
Beech Rd DT3 46 A4
Beverley Rd DT3 46 B5
Bincombe La DT3 46 B1
Bincombe Rise DT3 46 C6
Blackberry La DT3 46 B6
Brambling Clo DT3 46 B4
Bridlebank Way DT3 46 A5
Brisbane Rd DT3 46 C6
Broadlands Rd DT3 46 A6
Broadwey Clo DT3 46 B4
Brookton La DT3 46 C5
Buddleia Clo DT3 46 D6
Camedown Clo DT3 46 C5
Canberra Cres DT3 46 C5
Canberra Rd DT3 46 C6
Castlemaine Rd DT3 46 D6
Chaffinch Clo DT3 46 C5
Chapel La DT3 46 A3
Church St DT3 46 A2
Clayton Clo DT3 46 C5
Clivia Clo DT3 46 D6
Coppice Ct DT3 46 A6
Court Rd DT3 46 A6
Culliford Way DT3 46 C5
Dahlia Clo DT3 46 D6
Darwin Clo DT3 46 C6
Dorchester Rd DT3 46 A5
Elwell St DT3 46 A2
Fieldfare Clo DT3 46 B5
Firecrest Clo DT3 46 B4
Freesia Clo DT3 46 D6
Geelong Clo DT3 46 C6
Georgian Clo DT3 46 A5
Gladstone Clo DT3 46 A5
Goldcrest Clo DT3 46 B5
Hamilton Clo DT3 46 D6
Hillfield Clo DT3 46 A4
Icen La DT3 46 B4
Jenner Way DT3 46 C5
Jestys Av DT3 46 A4
Jordan Way DT3 46 B4
Juniper Way DT3 46 A5
Kestrel Vw DT3 46 B5
Kimberley Clo DT3 46 C6
Knoll Rise DT3 46 D6
Laurel La DT3 46 A3
Linnet Clo DT3 46 B4
Little Hill DT3 46 A5
Little Mead DT3 46 A5
Littlemoor Rd DT3 46 A4
Lorton La DT3 46 A6
Louviers Rd DT3 46 C5
Magnolia Clo DT3 46 D6
Meadow Vw Rd DT3 46 B4
Merlin Av Nth DT3 46 A5
Merlin Av Sth DT3 46 A5
Merredin Clo DT3 46 C5

Miles Gdns DT3 46 A3
Mill St DT3 46 A5
Nightingale Dri DT3 46 B4
Nottington La DT3 46 A6
Nuthatch Clo DT3 46 C5
Old Roman Rd DT3 46 A1
Old Station Rd DT3 46 A4
Park Ct DT3 46 D6
Pemberton Clo DT3 46 C5
Poplar Clo DT3 46 C5
Primula Clo DT3 46 D6
Prospect Pl DT3 46 A2
Redpoll Clo DT3 46 B4
Reedling Clo DT3 46 B5
Regency Dri DT3 46 A4
Ridgeway DT3 46 A2
Ridgeway Hill DT3 46 A2
Robin Clo DT3 46 B4
Rompathon Clo DT3 46 C5
St Helier Av DT3 46 A5
St Julien Cres DT3 46 A5
St Lawrence Rd DT3 46 A3
Sanderling Clo DT3 46 B5
Selwyn Clo DT3 46 C5
Shortlands Rd DT3 46 A3
Springfield Cres DT3 46 A5
Springfield Rd DT3 46 A5
Stonechat Clo DT3 46 B4
Stottingway St DT3 46 A3
The Doves DT3 46 C5
The Finches DT3 46 B5
The Grove DT3 46 A3
The Orchard DT3 46 A6
The Spinney DT3 46 A4
The Woodpeckers DT3 46 C5
Turnstone Clo DT3 46 B5
Victoria Av DT3 46 A3
Watery La DT3 46 A4
Wentworth Clo DT3 46 D6
Westlake Rd DT3 46 A4
Weyview Cres DT3 46 A4
Wheatear Clo DT3 46 B4
Windsor Rd DT3 46 A5

VERWOOD

Acacia Av BH31 47 F3
Acorn Cotts BH31 47 B1
Acorn Way BH31 47 B2
Aggis Farm BH31 47 B2
Albion Way BH31 47 A2
Aspen Dri BH31 47 E2
Badger Way BH31 47 C3
Bakers Farm Rd BH31 47 B1
Barberry Way BH31 47 F3
Beech Clo BH31 47 C3
Belmont Clo BH31 47 C3
Berkeley Clo BH31 47 C3
Bessemer Clo BH31 47 F4
Bingham Clo BH31 47 D4
Bingham Dri BH31 47 D4
Bingham Rd BH31 47 D4
Bitterne Way BH31 47 D3
Black Hill BH31 47 D2
Black Moor Rd BH31 47 A4
Blackthorn Way BH31 47 E3
Brickyard La BH31 47 A1
Bridleways BH31 47 C3
Bridport Rd BH31 47 C3
Brock Way BH31 47 B1
Brook Dri BH31 47 F4
Brunel Clo BH31 47 F4
Bugdens La BH31 47 C2
Burley Clo BH31 47 B3
Burn Clo BH31 47 E4
Burnbake Rd BH31 47 C3
Caradon Pl BH31 47 A1
Cartref Clo BH31 47 C3
Cheviot Way BH31 47 C2
Chiltern Dri BH31 47 C2
Church Hill BH31 47 B2
Churchfield BH31 47 B2
Claylake Dri BH31 47 D3
Compton Clo BH31 47 C1
Coniston Clo BH31 47 B3
Coopers La BH31 47 B1
Copse Rd BH31 47 C2
Coronation Clo BH31 47 C3
Coronation Rd BH31 47 C3
Cotswold Clo BH31 47 C3
Crane Clo BH31 47 B2
Crane Dri BH31 47 B2
Crescent Rd BH31 47 D2
Dewlands Pk BH31 47 B1

Dewlands Rd BH31 47 A2
Dewlands Way BH31 47 A2
Does La BH31 47 A2
Eastworth Rd BH31 47 A1
Ebblake Ind Est BH31 47 F3
Edmondsham Rd BH31 47 B1
Enterprise Park BH31 47 F3
Fairwood Rd BH31 47 E3
Fayrewood Ct BH31 47 C1
Field Pl BH31 47 B1
Firs Glen Rd BH31 47 C3
Forest La BH31 47 B2
Forge La BH31 47 A3
Foxes Clo BH31 47 C3
Foxhills BH31 47 E2
Glenwood Rd BH31 47 B3
Gorse Knoll Dri BH31 47 B1
Hainault Dri BH31 47 D2
Hayward Cres BH31 47 B3
Hayward Way BH31 47 A3
Haywards Farm Clo
BH31 47 B3
Hazelwood Dri BH31 47 E4
Heathlands Rd BH31 47 D4
Hillmeadow BH31 47 D2
Hillside Rd BH31 47 C1
Holly Gro BH31 47 A3
Holm Oak Clo BH31 47 B1
Home Farm Rd BH31 47 B2
Home Farm Way BH31 47 B2
Horton Way BH31 47 A3
Howard Rd BH31 47 C2
Howe La BH31 47 B3
Hunters Clo BH31 47 F3
Jenner Clo BH31 47 B1
Jessica Av BH31 47 A2
Keswick Way BH31 47 B3
Kiln Way BH31 47 F4
Laburnum Clo BH31 47 F3
Lake Rd BH31 47 D4
Lancaster Dri BH31 47 B3
Lavender Clo BH31 47 F3
Liederbach Dri BH31 47 F4
Little Dewlands BH31 47 A2
Lombardy Clo BH31 47 E2
Magnolia Clo BH31 47 F4
Mandalay Clo BH31 47 B3
Manor Gdns BH31 47 C2
Manor La BH31 47 C3
Manor Rd BH31 47 B2
Manor Way BH31 47 C2
Margards La BH31 47 A3
Meadow Ct BH31 47 D4
Meadow Gro BH31 47 D3
Meadow Way BH31 47 D3
Mendip Clo BH31 47 C3
Mendip Rd BH31 47 C3
Merryfield Clo BH31 47 C2
Moneyfly Rd BH31 47 E3
Monmouth Clo BH31 47 E4
Monmouth Dri BH31 47 D4
Montrose Clo BH31 47 D2
Moorlands Rd BH31 47 C1
Newtown La BH31 47 D3
Newtown Rd BH31 47 C3
Nightingale Clo BH31 47 D3
Noon Gdns BH31 47 E2
Noon Hill Dri BH31 47 E2
Noon Hill Rd BH31 47 E2
Oaklands Clo BH31 47 B2
Oaks Mead BH31 47 C2
Old Sawmill Clo BH31 47 A2
Orchard Ct BH31 47 D3
Otter Clo BH31 47 D3
Owls Rd BH31 47 D3
Paddock Gro BH31 47 D3
Park Dri BH31 47 B1
Peel Clo BH31 47 B1
Pennine Way BH31 47 C3
Penrith Clo BH31 47 B3
Pine View Clo BH31 47 A2
Pine View Rd BH31 47 A2
Pine Wk BH31 47 E3
Potterne Way BH31 47 D4
Potterne Way Ct BH31 47 F4
Purbeck Dri BH31 47 C3
Raymond Clo BH31 47 E2
Redmans Vw BH31 47 A2
Ringwood Rd BH31 47 C1
Roseberry Clo BH31 47 F3
Rowan Dri BH31 47 E4
St Michaels Clo BH31 47 C3
St Michaels Rd BH31 47 C3
St Stephens La BH31 47 D2
Sandy La BH31 47 D2
School Clo BH31 47 D2

Shard Clo BH31 47 D2
Sherwood Dri BH31 47 E2
Shetland Vw BH31 47 D2
Shires Mead BH31 47 D2
Sleepbrook Clo BH31 47 B2
Southernhay Rd BH31 47 E2
Spring Clo BH31 47 C3
Springfield Clo BH31 47 C3
Springfield Rd BH31 47 C3
Squirrel Walk BH31 47 C3
Stagswood BH31 47 A2
Stanley Clo BH31 47 D3
Starlight Farm Clo
BH31 47 D1
Station Rd BH31 47 A1
Strathmore Dri BH31 47 D2
Summer Fields BH31 47 B4
Taylor Way BH31 47 D2
The Chase BH31 47 E2
The Curlews BH31 47 D3
The Forelle Centre
BH31 47 F4
The Forestside BH31 47 F3
The Grove BH31 47 C3
The Kingfishers BH31 47 D3
The Lea BH31 47 D3
The Mews BH31 47 D4
The Oaks BH31 47 B1
Thomas Lockyer Clo
BH31 47 B2
Thorne Clo BH31 47 B2
Verne Rd BH31 47 D3
Verwood Ind Est BH31 47 D2
Vicarage Rd BH31 47 C1
West Clo BH31 47 A2
Whitebeam Way BH31 47 E3
Wisteria Dri BH31 47 F4
Woodland Clo BH31 47 B1
Woodlinken Clo BH31 47 E4
Woodlinken Dri BH31 47 E4
Woodlinken Way BH31 47 E4
Woodpecker Clo BH31 47 C3

WAREHAM

Abbots Quay BH20 48 B6
Admirals Way BH20 48 C3
Anglebury Business Park
BH20 48 B4
Avon Dri BH20 48 B3
Barnes Rd BH20 48 A6
Bells Orchard La BH20 48 C5
Bere Rd BH20 48 A3
Bestwall Rd BH20 48 C5
Bestwall Cres BH20 48 C6
Bonnets La BH20 48 B5
Bourne Dri BH20 48 A3
Brixeys La BH20 48 B5
Bryn Rd BH20 48 D1
Burns Rd BH20 48 A3
Carey Clo BH20 48 A4
Carey Rd BH20 48 A4
Carrion La BH20 48 B5
Causeway Clo BH20 48 B4
Church Ct BH20 48 C6
Church Grn BH20 48 B6
Church La BH20 48 C6
Church St BH20 48 C6
Churchwood Ct*, St
Michaels Rd BH20 48 B5
Connigar La BH20 48 A5
Coopers Clo BH20 48 B5
Courtenay Clo BH20 48 C3
Cow La BH20 48 B5
Daniel Dri BH20 48 B3
Dollins La BH20 48 B5
Drax Av BH20 48 B3
East St BH20 48 B6
East Walls BH20 48 C6
Edward Cres BH20 48 B5
Egdon Rd BH20 48 A3
Elwood Clo BH20 48 D1
Encombe Rd BH20 48 B6
Fairway Dri BH20 48 A3
Filleul Rd BH20 48 D1
Folly La BH20 48 B5
Forest Edge Rd BH20 48 C2
Frome Rd BH20 48 A6
Gore Hill BH20 48 C1
Great Ovens Dri BH20 48 B2
Hardy Rd BH20 48 A6
Hobbs Clo BH20 48 B4
Howards La BH20 48 B5
Humber Chase BH20 48 A4

Justin Business Pk
BH20 48 B4
Johns Rd BH20 48 B4
Kennington Sq*,
North St BH20 48 B5
Keysworth Dri BH20 48 D1
Knightstons Clo*,
East St BH20 48 B6
Leanne Business Pk
BH20 48 C4
Mellstock Cres BH20 48 A4
Middle Bere Dri BH20 48 A3
Miles Av BH20 48 D1
Mill La BH20 48 B5
Mistover Rd BH20 48 A4
Monmouth Rd BH20 48 A5
Morden Rd BH20 48 C1
Moretons La BH20 48 B5
Mount Pleasant BH20 48 B5
New St BH20 48 B6
Norden Dri BH20 48 A3
North Bestwall Rd
BH20 48 C5
North Causeway BH20 48 B4
North St BH20 48 B5
North Walls BH20 48 B5
Northmoor Way BH20 48 A3
Northport Dri BH20 48 B3
Pound La BH20 48 B6
Rodgett Cres BH20 48 D1
Ropers La BH20 48 D1
Ryan Business Pk
BH20 48 C3
Ryan Clo BH20 48 B4
St Helens Rd BH20 48 D1
St Johns Hill BH20 48 B6
St Martins Clo BH20 48 B5
St Martins La BH20 48 B5
St Martins Rd BH20 48 D1
St Marys Clo BH20 48 A4
St Michaels Rd BH20 48 B5
Sandford La BH20 48 A4
Sandford Rd BH20 48 B4
Seven Barrows Rd
BH20 48 A3
Shatters Hill BH20 48 B5
Shaw Dri BH20 48 C2
Sherford Clo BH20 48 B3
Sherford Dri BH20 48 B3
Shirley Rd BH20 48 A6
South Causeway BH20 48 B6
South St BH20 48 B6
Stockley Rd BH20 48 A3
Stour Dri BH20 48 B3
Stowell Cres BH20 48 A6
Streche Rd BH20 48 B5
Tamlin St BH20 48 D1
Tanners La BH20 48 B5
Tantinoby La BH20 48 B3
Tarrant Rd BH20 48 B3
The Beeches BH20 48 D1
The Croft BH20 48 C5
The Quay BH20 48 B6
Tinkers La BH20 48 B5
Trent Dri BH20 48 A3
Trinity Clo*,
Abbots Quay BH20 48 B6
Trinity La BH20 48 B6
Tyneham Clo BH20 48 D1
Walls View Rd BH20 48 A4
Wareham By-Pass
BH20 48 A5
Wellstead Rd BH20 48 A4
Wessex Oval BH20 48 A4
West Mill Cres BH20 48 A4
West St BH20 48 B6
West Walls BH20 48 B5
Westminster Rd BH20 48 A4
Westport Rd BH20 48 B6
Willow Way BH20 48 A3
Worgret Rd BH20 48 A4
Wyatts La BH20 48 C6

WEST LULWORTH

Beech Clo BH20 49 C1
Bindon Clo BH20 49 C1
Bindon Rd BH20 49 B2
Chestnut Ct*,
Moreys Clo BH20 49 C1
Church Hill BH20 49 B1
Farm Rd BH20 49 C1
Main Rd BH20 49 B2
Moreys Clo BH20 49 C2

School La BH20 49 B1
Shepherds Way BH20 49 C1
Sunnyside Rd BH20 49 B2
The Launches BH20 49 B1
Vale Rd BH20 49 C1
West Lulworth Farm*,
Farm Rd BH20 49 C1

WEST MOORS

Abbey Rd BH22 54 C6
Abbotts Way BH22 54 D6
Arnold Clo BH22 54 B3
Arnold Rd BH22 54 B3
Ashurst Rd BH22 54 A3
Avon Rd BH22 54 B5
Beechwood Rd BH22 54 C5
Belle Vue Gro BH22 54 C4
Berkeley Ct*,
Moorside Rd BH22 54 B4
Birch Gro BH22 54 A4
Blackfield La BH22 54 B3
Bond Av BH22 54 A3
Braeside Rd BH22 54 B3
Bramble Ct BH22 54 A4
Bridges Clo BH22 54 B5
Canterbury Clo BH22 54 B5
Castleman Ct BH22 54 A3
Charnwood Clo BH22 54 B4
Compton Cres BH22 54 D5
Condor Clo BH22 54 D1
Denewood Copse
BH22 54 A3
Denewood Rd BH22 54 A2
Edgemoor Rd BH22 54 D5
Elmhurst Rd BH22 54 C5
Elmhurst Way BH22 54 C5
Farm Rd BH22 54 A4
Ferndown By-Pass
BH22 54 A6
Fernside Rd BH22 54 B4
Fir Clo BH22 54 B3
Firs Glen Rd BH22 54 B4
Forest Rd BH22 54 C3
Garden Court Cotts
BH22 54 A3
Glenwood Clo BH22 54 B4
Glenwood La BH22 54 B4
Glenwood Rd BH22 54 B4
Glenwood Way BH22 54 B4
Gundrymoor Trading Est
BH22 54 B1
Hardy Clo BH22 54 C5
Hardy Rd BH22 54 C5
Harrison Way BH22 54 B3
Hazel Dri BH22 54 A6
Heatherdown Rd BH22 54 D5
Heatherdown Way
BH22 54 D5
Heathfield Rd BH22 54 C5
Heathfield Way BH22 54 C5
Heston Way BH22 54 A3
Highfield Rd BH22 54 A2
Holly Clo BH22 54 A4
Jimmy Brown Av
BH22 54 B1
Kingfisher Clo BH22 54 B1
Kings Clo BH22 54 A5
Knightstone Gro BH22 54 A4
Maloren Way BH22 54 C5
Mannington Way
BH22 54 A4
Mary La BH22 54 A4
Merino Way BH22 54 C5
Milford Clo BH22 54 C4
Moorlands Rise BH22 54 C3
Monks Clo BH22 54 D6
Moorlands Rd BH22 54 B5
Moorside Rd BH22 54 B5
Newcombe Rd BH22 54 B5
Newmans Clo BH22 54 B1
Newmans La BH22 54 A1
Oakhurst Clo BH22 54 B4
Oakhurst La BH22 54 C4
Oakhurst Rd BH22 54 B5
Old Barn Farm Rd
BH22 54 D1
Park Way BH22 54 B1
Payne Clo BH22 54 B1
Penn Ct BH22 54 A4
Pennington Clo BH22 54 A5
Pennington Cres BH22 54 A5
Pennington Rd BH22 54 A5
Pinehurst Pk BH22 54 C6

Pinehurst Rd BH22 54 B5
Priory Gdns BH22 54 C6
Priory Rd BH22 54 C6
Pullman Ct BH22 54 A4
Queens Clo BH22 54 A5
Ringwood Rd BH22 54 D6
Ritchie Pl BH22 54 A3
Riverside Rd BH22 54 A4
Sarum Av BH22 54 B2
Shaftesbury Clo BH22 54 C4
Shaftesbury Rd BH22 54 B3
Shirley Clo BH22 54 B4
Southdown Way BH22 54 B5
Southern Av BH22 54 C5
Spinners Clo BH22 54 A5
Station Rd BH22 54 A5
Summercroft Way
BH22 54 B3
Teasel Way BH22 54 B5
The Avenue BH22 54 A3
Uplands Clo BH22 54 D6
Uplands Rd BH22 54 C4
Weavers Clo BH22 54 B5
West Moors Rd BH22 54 A2
Woodside Rd BH22 54 A2
Woolslope Clo BH22 54 B5
Woolslope Gdns BH22 54 B5
Woolslope Rd BH22 54 B5

WEYMOUTH

Abbotsbury Rd DT4 52 C2
Acacia Clo DT4 50 B4
Adelaide Cres DT4 52 C1
Albert St*,
Park St DT4 53 F1
Alexandra Gdns DT4 53 F2
Alexandra Rd,
Charlestown DT4 52 A1
Alexandra Rd,
Weymouth DT4 50 D5
All Saints Rd DT4 52 B4
Alma Rd DT4 53 E1
Almond Gro DT4 50 B4
Ambleside DT3 50 B3
Appletree Clo DT3 50 C2
Aragon Clo DT4 52 D4
Argyle Rd DT4 50 D4
Arlington DT4 50 B5
Ashton Rd DT4 52 D2
Astrid Way DT4 51 E6
Augusta Pl DT 53 F2
Avenue Rd DT4 51 E6
Avocet Clo DT4 52 D6
Aynsley Ct DT4 50 C6
Barclay Rd DT4 52 D1
Barley Way DT4 53 F4
Barnhaven Clo DT4 52 D3
Barrack Rd DT4 53 F2
Barrow Rise DT4 52 B4
Bath St DT4 53 E1
Baycliff Rd DT4 52 C2
Beach Clo DT4 51 E5
Beachdown Way DT3 51 F2
Beachview Clo DT4 52 B4
Beaulieu DT4 50 B4
Beaumont Av DT4 50 D4
Bedford Rd DT4 50 A6
Belfield Clo DT4 52 D3
Belfield Pk Av DT4 52 C3
Belfield Pk Dri DT4 52 C4
Belgrave DT4 50 B4
Belgrave Cotts DT4 50 D4
Belle Vue Rd DT4 53 E4
Belmont St DT4 53 F3
Belvidere DT4 51 E6
Ben Nevis Rd DT4 52 D3
Benville Rd DT4 52 B2
Bincleaves Rd DT4 53 E3
Birch Way DT3 51 F2
Blenheim Rd DT3 50 C1
Bodkin La DT3 51 G2
Bohays Dri DT4 52 B5
Boleyn Cres DT4 52 D5
Bond St DT4 53 F1
Boulton Clo DT4 52 C4
Bowleaze Coveway
DT3 51 G2
Brackendown Av DT3 51 F2
Bradford Rd DT4 52 D2
Briar Clo DT4 50 A5
Broadmeadow Rd DT4 52 C5
Broughton Cres DT4 52 C5

Brownlow St DT4 50 D6
Brunswick Ter DT4 51 E6
Bryants La DT4 52 B4
Bryn Rd DT4 52 C2
Budmouth Av DT3 51 G2
Buxton Clo DT4 52 C4
Buxton Rd DT4 52 C4
Caledonian Clo DT4 50 D5
Cambridge Rd DT4 52 A1
Camp Rd DT4 52 A5
Campion Clo DT4 51 E4
Canterbury Clo DT4 52 B1
Carisbrooke DT4 50 B5
Carlton Rd Nth DT4 50 D6
Carlton Rd Sth DT4 50 D6
Caroline Pl*,
  Park St DT4 53 F2
Carrington Clo DT4 52 D4
Cassiobury Rd DT4 50 D5
Castle Hill Rd DT4 52 B4
Causeway DT4 50 A3
Causeway Cotts DT4 50 A3
Celandine Clo DT4 50 D4
Chafeys Av DT4 50 A5
Chamberlaine Rd DT4 52 B4
Chapelhay St DT4 53 E2
Charles St DT4 50 D6
Chartwell DT4 50 B4
Chelmsford St DT4 50 D6
Chelwood Gate DT4 52 A1
Cherry Way DT3 51 G2
Chesil Vw DT4 52 B5
Chestnut Pl DT3 50 C2
Chickerell Rd DT4 52 A1
Chickerell Ter DT4 52 C2
Church Knapp DT4 52 C4
Churchill Clo DT4 52 B4
Clare Av DT3 52 A2
Clarence Rd DT4 52 A2
Clarendon Av DT3 50 C1
Clearmount Rd DT4 52 D4
Cleveland Av DT4 50 D4
Cleves Clo DT4 52 D5
Clifton Pl*, Gloucester
  Mews DT4 53 F2
Clive Ter DT4 52 D1
Cobham Dri DT4 52 B1
Cockles La DT4 52 A4
Colchester Way DT4 52 B1
College La DT4 51 E5
Collins La DT4 52 B3
Comet Clo DT4 52 B3
Commercial Rd DT4 53 F1
Concorde Clo DT4 52 A3
Conifer Way DT4 50 B4
Coniston Cres DT3 50 C3
Connaught Rd DT4 52 D3
Coombe Av DT4 50 D4
Corfe Rd DT4 50 B2
Cornwall Clo DT4 52 C1
Coronation Cres DT3 50 C3
Coronation Rd DT3 50 C3
Corporation Rd DT4 52 B1
Corscombe Clo DT4 53 E1
Courtauld Dri DT4 52 C4
Cove Pl*,
Cove Row DT4 53 F2
Cove Row DT4 53 F2
Cove St*,
Cove Row DT4 53 F2
Coveway DT3 51 G2
Cranford Av DT4 51 E5
Creech Way DT3 50 B2
Crescent St DT4 51 E6
Crispins Clo DT4 52 B4
Cromwell Rd DT4 52 D1
Cross Rd DT4 52 D3
Cumberland Dri DT4 52 A1
Cunningham Clo DT4 52 B4
Custom House Quay*,
Maiden St DT4 53 F2
Dale Av DT4 50 D4
Davenport Ct DT4 53 E1
Dawlish Cres DT4 52 D5
Dennis Rd DT4 52 C2
Derby St DT4 50 D6
Derwent Rd DT4 53 E3
Devenish Clo DT4 53 E3
Devenish Gdns DT4 53 E3
Devon Rd DT4 50 B6
Doncaster Rd DT4 52 C6
Dorchester Rd DT4 52 C1
Dorset Clo DT4 52 C1
Dorset Rd DT4 52 C2
Douglas Rd DT4 52 C6
Doulton Clo DT4 53 E1

Dover Rd DT4 52 C6
Down Clo DT4 52 C5
Down Rd DT4 52 D3
Dumbarton Rd DT4 52 C6
Dundee Rd DT4 52 C6
Eadon Clo DT3 51 G1
East St DT4 53 F2
East Wyld Rd DT4 52 C1
Eastdown Av DT3 51 F2
Eastdown Gdns DT3 51 F2
Ebor Rd DT4 52 B4
Edward St*,
  Park St DT4 53 F1
Edwardsville*,
  Rodwell Av DT4 53 E3
Elm Clo DT3 51 G3
Elveroakes Way DT4 52 C6
Elwell Manor Gdns
  DT4 53 E3
Emerson Rd DT4 52 D2
Emmadale Clo DT4 52 D1
Emmadale Rd DT4 52 D1
Enkworth Rd DT3 51 G1
Esplanade*,
  Royal Cres DT4 51 E6
Essex Rd DT4 52 D1
Everdene Dri DT3 52 A2
Everest Rd DT4 52 D3
Fairclose DT4 52 D3
Faircross Av DT4 52 D3
Fairview Rd DT4 52 C5
Farm Clo DT4 50 B5
Faversham DT4 50 B4
Ferndale Rd DT4 50 D4
Fernhill Av DT4 50 D4
Field Barn Dri DT4 50 A5
Fleetview Rd DT4 52 B5
Fossett Way DT4 52 B4
Franchise St DT4 53 E2
Francis Rd DT4 52 C2
Franklin Clo DT4 52 D1
Franklin Rd DT4 52 C1
Fraser Av DT4 52 A2
Freemantle Rd DT4 52 A3
Furzy Clo DT3 51 G1
Gallwey Rd DT4 52 C5
Garibaldi Row DT4 52 D2
Glebe Clo DT4 52 D3
Glen Av DT4 52 D2
Glendinning Av DT4 50 D5
Glenmore Rd DT4 50 B6
Gloucester Mews DT4 53 F1
Gloucester Row DT4 53 F1
Gloucester St DT4 53 F1
Goldcroft Av DT4 50 C6
Goldcroft Rd DT4 50 B5
Gordon Cres DT4 52 A2
Gordon Row DT4 53 E2
Goss Pl DT4 50 C6
Governors La*,
  East St DT4 53 F2
Grafton Av DT4 50 A4
Granby Clo DT4 52 B1
Granby Ind Est DT4 52 A1
Granby Way DT4 50 A5
Grange Rd DT4 51 E5
Granville Rd DT4 52 D4
Grasmere Clo DT3 50 C4
Grasmere Rd DT3 50 C4
Grays DT4 50 B4
Great George St DT4 53 F1
Great Western Ter DT4 50 A4
Green La DT4 52 D4
Greenhill DT4 51 E5
Greenway Clo DT3 50 C2
Greenway Rd DT4 50 C2
Grosvenor Rd DT4 50 D5
Grove Av DT4 52 D1
Grove Ter DT4 52 D1
Gypsy La DT4 52 D2
Hammond Av DT4 50 A4
Hanover Rd DT4 50 D5
Hardwick St DT4 53 E2
Hardy Av DT4 52 C2
Hawthorn Clo DT4 50 B4
Haymoor Av DT4 51 F2
Haywards Av DT4 50 D3
Hazeldown Av DT4 50 A6
Helen La*,
  East St DT4 53 F2
Henry Clo DT4 50 D3
Herbert Pl DT4 53 F2
Hereford Rd DT4 52 B2
Heron Clo DT3 51 G2
Hetherly Rd DT3 50 D3

High Down DT3 51 F2
High St DT4 52 B4
High West St DT4 53 E2
Highland Rd DT4 52 D1
Hill La DT4 53 F2
Hillbourne Clo DT4 52 C5
Hillbourne Rd DT4 52 C5
Hillcrest Rd DT4 52 D5
Holland Clo DT4 53 E1
Holland Rd DT4 53 E1
Holly Rd DT4 52 D1
Holme Clo DT3 50 B2
Holyrood Ter DT4 52 D1
Hope Sq DT4 53 F2
Hope St DT4 53 F2
Hornbeam Clo DT4 50 B4
Horsford St DT4 53 F3
Howard Clo DT4 52 D5
Icen Rd DT3 50 C3
Ilchester Rd DT4 53 E1
James St DT4 52 D1
Jasmine Way DT4 52 B3
John St*,
  West St DT4 53 E1
Jubilee Clo DT4 50 D6
Jubilee Enterprise
  Centre DT4 50 D5
Jubilee Retail Pk DT4 50 D6
Kayes Clo DT4 52 C4
Kellaway Ter DT4 52 D1
Kempston Rd DT4 53 E3
Kenilworth DT4 50 B4
Kenmoor Clo DT3 51 F2
Kent Clo DT4 52 A1
Khartoum Rd DT4 53 E4
Kimmeridge Clo DT3 50 B2
King St DT4 50 D6
Kingfisher Clo DT4 52 C6
Kings Rd DT3 50 C3
Kingsbere Rd DT3 51 G1
Kirtleton Av DT4 50 D5
Kitchener Rd DT4 52 C1
Knightsdale Rd DT4 52 D2
Laburnum Clo DT4 50 B4
Lakeside Gdns DT3 50 C3
Lakeside Wk DT4 53 E1
Lancaster Rd DT3 50 B1
Lanehouse Rocks Rd
  DT4 52 B1
Lanehouses Clo DT4 52 B2
Langton Av DT4 52 C6
Lansdowne Sq DT4 52 D3
Larkspur Clo DT 51 E4
Lea Rd DT4 52 B4
Leamington Rd DT4 52 B2
Leeds Cres DT4 52 B2
Lennox St DT4 50 D6
Lessingham Av DT4 52 C6
Lichfield Rd DT4 52 B2
Lincoln Rd DT4 52 B2
Lindens Clo DT4 50 C4
Links Rd DT4 50 B6
Littleview Rd DT4 52 B2
Liverpool Rd DT4 52 C2
Lodge Way DT4 52 C4
Lodmoor Av DT3 50 D3
Lomond Dri DT4 50 D3
Longcroft Rd DT4 52 C1
Longfield Rd DT4 53 E3
Lookout DT4 53 F3
Love La DT4 53 E2
Lower Bond St DT4 53 E1
Lower St Albans St
  DT4 53 E2
Lower St Edmund St*,
  St Nicholas St DT4 53 E2
Ludlow Rd DT4 52 B2
Lydwell Clo DT4 52 D4
Lymes Clo DT4 52 B4
Lynch La DT4 52 A2
Lynch Rd DT4 52 B2
Lyndale Rd DT4 52 C6
Lyndhurst Rd DT4 50 D5
Lynmoor Rd DT4 51 E4
McKay Clo DT4 52 A2
McKay Way DT4 52 A2
Maiden St DT4 53 F2
Maple Clo DT3 51 H1
Malvern Ter DT4 52 C2
Mandeville Clo DT4 52 A4
Mandeville Rd DT4 52 A4
Manor Rd DT4 50 C2
Marina Gdns DT4 52 D3
Market St DT4 53 F2
Markham Av DT4 52 C2
Marlborough Av DT4 52 C5

Marlow Rd DT4 53 F3
Marquis Clo DT4 52 A2
Marsh Rd DT4 53 E2
Martleaves Clo DT4 52 C4
Maycroft Rd DT4 53 E3
Mayfield Clo DT4 50 A4
Mead Rd DT4 50 A4
Melbourne St DT4 52 C1
Melbury Rd DT4 53 E1
Melcombe Av DT4 51 E5
Melstock Av DT3 51 G1
Mercery Rd DT3 50 C3
Merley Rd DT4 52 C6
Milton Clo DT4 50 D4
Milton Cres DT4 50 D4
Milton Rd DT4 52 D1
Milton Ter DT4 50 D4
Minton Pl DT4 50 C6
Mitchell St*,
  East St DT4 53 F3
Monmouth Rd DT3 50 D3
Moordown Av DT3 51 F2
Moorside Av DT4 51 E4
Moorside Clo DT4 51 E4
Mount Pleasant Av Nth
  DT3 50 C2
Mount Pleasant Av Sth
  DT3 50 C3
Mount Pleasant
  Business Pk DT3 50 D2
Mount St DT4 52 C4
Mountbatten Clo DT4 52 B4
Mulberry Ter*,
  School St DT4 53 F2
Netherton Rd DT4 53 E3
New Bond St DT4 53 E1
New Clo DT4 52 B5
New Clo Gdns DT4 53 E3
New Rd DT4 53 E2
New St DT4 53 E2
Newberry Gdns DT4 53 F2
Newberry Rd DT4 53 F2
Newstead Rd DT4 53 E2
Newtons Rd DT4 53 F3
Norfolk Rd DT4 52 B1
North Quay DT4 53 E2
North Rd DT4 52 B4
Norwich Rd DT4 53 E3
Nothe Parade DT4 53 F2
Nothe Walk DT4 53 F2
Nutgrove Av DT4 52 A3
Oak Way DT3 51 G2
Oakbury Dri DT3 51 G2
Oakley Pl DT4 53 E3
Old Castle Rd DT4 53 E5
Old Parish La DT4 52 C1
Orchard Dri DT3 51 G1
Orion Rd DT4 53 E3
Osprey Rd DT4 52 C6
Overbury Clo DT4 52 A2
Overcombe Cotts DT3 51 H2
Overcombe Rd DT4 51 H1
Overlands Rd DT4 52 B4
Park La DT4 50 D5
Park Mead Rd DT4 52 C5
Park St DT4 53 E1
Parr Way DT4 53 E4
Penny St*,
  Hardwick St DT4 50 D6
Perth St DT4 52 C1
Pilgrims Way DT4 53 F2
Pinemoor Clo DT3 51 F2
Pirates La DT4 52 B5
Plover Dri DT4 52 C6
Poplar Clo DT4 50 A4
Portland Cres DT4 52 C5
Portland Rd DT4 52 C5
Portmore Gdns DT4 53 E3
Portwey Clo DT4 53 E3
Pottery La DT4 50 C6
Preston Beach Rd DT3 51 F3
Preston Rd DT3 51 G2
Pretoria Ter DT4 52 D2
Prince of Wales Rd
  DT4 52 D2
Princes Dri DT4 50 D4
Prospect Pl DT4 53 E2
Purbeck Clo DT4 52 D3
Queen St DT4 50 D6
Queens Rd DT3 50 C3
Queensland Rd DT4 52 C1
Quibo La DT4 52 B2
Radipole Ct DT4 52 C5
Radipole La DT4 52 B1
Radipole Park Dri DT4 50 C3
Radipole Ter DT4 50 D5

Ranelagh Rd DT4 50 D6
Raymond Rd DT4 52 A2
Rectory Way DT4 52 D3
Redcliff Vw DT4 53 F3
Reed View Clo DT4 50 B5
Ringstead Cres DT3 51 G2
Rochester Ct DT4 52 B1
Rocky Knap DT3 50 C3
Rodden Clo DT4 52 C4
Rodwell Av DT4 53 E3
Rodwell Rd DT4 53 E2
Rodwell St*,
  Rodwell Rd DT4 53 E3
Roman Clo DT3 50 C3
Roman Rd DT3 50 C3
Rosecroft Rd DT4 52 D1
Roundham Gdns DT4 52 C2
Roundhayes Clo DT4 52 C2
Rowan Clo DT4 50 B4
Rowland Ct DT4 51 E4
Royal Cres DT4 51 E6
Royal Ter DT4 53 F1
Russell Av DT4 52 C3
Rutland Rd DT4 50 B6
Ryemead La DT4 52 B5
Rylands La DT4 52 C4
St Alban St DT4 53 F2
St Andrews Av DT3 50 D3
St Annes Rd DT4 52 D5
St Davids Rd DT4 52 D5
St Georges Av DT4 51 E4
St Helens Rd DT4 52 A2
St Leonards Rd DT4 53 E3
St Martins Rd DT4 52 D4
St Marys St DT4 53 F2
St Michaels Ct DT4 52 D3
St Nicholas St DT4 53 E2
St Patricks Av DT4 52 A3
St Thomas St DT4 53 E2
Salisbury Rd DT4 53 E1
Samphire Clo DT4 50 D4
Sandbourne Rd DT3 51 G1
Sandpiper Way DT4 52 C6
School Ct DT4 53 F1
Seamoor Clo DT4 51 F2
Sedgefield Clo DT4 52 D1
Shears Rd DT4 50 D3
Shirecroft Rd DT4 52 C1
Short Rd DT4 52 C1
Shrubbery La DT4 52 B4
Somerset Rd DT4 50 B6
Sorrel Clo DT4 51 E4
Souter Way DT3 50 D2
South Par DT4 53 F2
South Rd DT4 52 B5
Southcroft Rd DT4 52 B3
Southdown Av DT3 51 F2
Southdown Rd DT4 52 D4
Southfield Av DT4 50 D4
Southill Gdn Dri DT4 50 B4
Southlands Rd DT4 52 D4
Southview Rd DT4 52 C1
Spa Av DT4 50 C3
Spa Rd DT4 50 B3
Spring Av DT4 53 E3
Spring Clo DT4 53 E3
Spring Gdns DT4 53 E3
Spring La DT4 53 F2
Spring Rd DT4 53 F3
Stainforth Clo DT4 52 B1
Stanley St DT4 50 D6
Stavordale Ct DT4 53 E1
Stavordale Rd DT4 53 E1
Steeple Clo DT3 50 B2
Stirling Rd DT4 50 D4
Stoborough Clo DT3 50 C2
Stoke Rd DT4 52 C5
Stonehill Ct DT4 52 B5
Studland Way DT3 50 B2
Sudan Rd DT4 53 E4
Sundew Clo DT4 51 E4
Sunningdale Rise DT3 51 G1
Sunnyside Rd DT4 52 C5
Sussex Rd DT4 50 B6
Sutcliffe Av DT4 50 A4
Swaffield Gdns DT4 52 C4
Swannery Bri DT4 53 E1
Sycamore Rd DT4 50 B4
Sydney St DT4 52 C1
Symonds Clo DT3 50 D3
Tecan Way DT4 52 A1
Teeling Rd DT4 52 A1
Tennyson Rd DT4 52 D2
Terminus St*,
  King St DT4 50 D6
The Cherries DT3 50 C2

The Maltings DT4 53 F3
The Rise DT4 50 A6
Thornhill Cres DT4 50 C6
Thornlow Clo DT4 52 D4
Tollerdown Rd DT4 52 B2
Trinity Ct*,
  Trinity Ter DT4 53 E2
Trinity Rd DT4 53 E2
Trinity St DT4 53 F2
Trinity Ter DT4 53 E2
Turton St*, Gloucester
  Mews DT4 53 F1
Tyneham Clo DT3 50 B2
Ullswater Cres DT4 50 B3
Underbarn Wk DT4 53 E4
Vanguard Av DT4 52 A3
Verne Clo DT4 53 E3
Verne Rd DT4 53 E3
Verne Way DT4 52 D3
Victoria Rd DT4 52 C5
Victoria St DT4 51 E6
Victoria Ter DT4 51 E6
Viscount Rd DT4 52 B3
Vulcan Clo DT4 52 A3
Walker Cres DT4 52 C6
Walpole St DT4 50 D6
Wardcliffe Rd DT4 52 D1
Warren Clo DT4 52 B2
Waverley Rd DT4 50 C4
Wedgwood Rd DT4 53 E1
Wellington Ct DT4 53 F2
Wesley St DT4 52 E1
Wessex Rd DT4 52 C1
West Bay Cres DT4 52 B5
West St DT4 50 D5
Westbourne Rd DT4 50 D5
Westdowne Clo DT4 52 B2
Westerhall Rd DT4 51 E5
Westham Rd DT4 53 E1
Westhaven DT4 52 B1
Westhill Clo DT4 52 B4
Westhill Rd DT4 52 B4
Weston Rd DT4 53 E2
Westwey Rd DT4 53 E2
Weymouth Bay Av
  DT4 50 D3
Weymouth Rd DT4 53 E1
Weymouth Way DT4 50 B3
Whitecross Dri DT4 52 D4
William St DT4 51 E6
Williams Av DT4 52 C5
Wilton Dri DT4 52 D3
Wiltshire Rd DT4 52 C1
Winchester Clo DT4 52 B1
Windermere Cres DT4 50 B3
Wingreen Clo DT3 51 H1
Winterbourne Copse
  DT4 52 D4
Winton Clo DT4 50 A4
Woodperton St*,
  Westham Rd DT4 53 E1
Wooland Gdns DT4 52 B4
Wyke Oliver Clo DT3 51 G1
Wyke Oliver Rd DT3 51 G1
Wyke Rd DT4 52 C4

Wyke Sq DT4 52 B4
Yarlands DT4 52 A1

WIMBORNE MINSTER

Allen Ct BH21 55 B3
Allen Rd BH21 55 C4
Allenview Rd BH21 55 C2
Ashdene Clo BH21 55 D3
Ashington La BH21 55 A5
Avenue Rd BH21 55 C4
Badbury Vw BH21 55 C2
Barnes Cres BH21 55 D4
Bartley Ct BH21 55 B3
Beaucroft La BH21 55 D2
Beaucroft Rd BH21 55 D2
Beaufort Dri BH21 55 C3
Beech Ct BH21 55 D4
Bells Ho BH21 55 C2
Birchdale Rd BH21 55 D3
Blind La BH21 55 C2
Boundary Dri BH21 55 C2
Bourne Ct BH21 55 C3
Broadway Gdns BH21 55 C4
Brook Rd BH21 55 D4
Burts Hill BH21 55 B2
Byron Rd BH21 55 C2
Cemetery Rd BH21 55 A3
Chapel La BH21 55 B2
Charles Keightley Ct
  BH21 55 D4
Chaucer Clo BH21 55 B2
Chene Rd BH21 55 D3
Cheriton Way BH21 55 C2
Church St BH21 55 B3
Churchill Rd BH21 55 D5
Cobbs Rd BH21 55 C4
Cobham Way BH21 55 D6
Cook Row BH21 55 B3
Coopercourt Leaze
  BH21 55 C4
Corn Market BH21 55 B3
Courtenay Dri BH21 55 C2
Cowdrys Fld BH21 55 B2
Cowgrove Rd BH21 55 A3
Cranborne Rd BH21 55 B2
Cranfield Av BH21 55 C3
Crescent Rd BH21 55 C4
Cromwell Rd BH21 55 D4
Crown Mead BH21 55 B3
Culverhayes Clo BH21 55 B2
Culverhayes Pl BH21 55 A2
Culverhayes Rd BH21 55 A2
Cuthburga Rd BH21 55 C3
Cuthbury Clo BH21 55 A3
Cuthbury Gdns BH21 55 A3
Days Ct BH21 55 D4
Deans Court La BH21 55 B4
Dean Gro BH21 55 D1
Derwentwater Rd
  BH21 55 C5
Dogdean BH21 55 B1

East Borough BH21 55 B2
East St BH21 55 B4
Eden Gro BH21 55 C4
Elizabeth Rd BH21 55 C3
Ethelbert Rd BH21 55 C4
Fairfield Rd BH21 55 C3
Farmers Walk BH21 55 B2
Flower Ct BH21 55 C4
Giddylake BH21 55 C2
Glendale Clo BH21 55 C2
Gordon Rd BH21 55 D4
Grammar School La
  BH21 55 B4
Greenclose La BH21 55 D3
Greenhays Rise BH21 55 C3
Greenhill Clo BH21 55 D2
Greenhill La BH21 55 D2
Greenhill Rd BH21 55 D2
Grenville Rd BH21 55 C4
Griffin Ct BH21 55 C5
Grove Rd BH21 55 C4
Gullivers Ct BH21 55 B3
Hamilton Ct BH21 55 B2
Hanham Rd BH21 55 B3
Hardy Cres BH21 55 D5
Harrier Dri BH21 55 D6
Helic Ho BH21 55 B3
High St BH21 55 B3
Highland Rd BH21 55 D2
Highland View Clo
  BH21 55 D2
Hornbeam Way BH21 55 D3
Ingram Walk BH21 55 C4
Julians Rd BH21 55 A4
King St BH21 55 B3
Knobcrook Rd BH21 55 B2
Lacy Clo BH21 55 C2
Lacy Dri BH21 55 C2
Legg La BH21 55 C3
Leigh Clo BH21 55 D3
Leigh Gdns BH21 55 D4
Leigh Rd BH21 55 C4
Lewens Clo BH21 55 C3
Lewens La BH21 55 C3
Livingstone Rd BH21 55 D4
Market Way BH21 55 C4
Marlborough Ct BH21 55 B3
Marlborough Pl BH21 55 C3
Meadow Ct BH21 55 C4
Melverley Gdns BH21 55 C3
Merley Ways BH21 55 C5
Mill La BH21 55 B3
Millstream Clo BH21 55 B4
Milton Rd BH21 55 B2
Minster Vw BH21 55 C3
Moray Ct BH21 55 B3
Netherwood Pl BH21 55 A3
New Borough Rd BH21 55 C4
Oakdene Clo BH21 55 D3
Oakley Hill BH21 55 C5
Oakley La BH21 55 D6
Oakley Rd BH21 55 D6
Old Highway Mews
  BH21 55 D4
Old Manor Clo BH21 55 D3

Old Rd BH21 55 A3
Onslow Gdns BH21 55 C2
Onslow Ho BH21 55 C2
Osborne Rd BH21 55 C4
Park La BH21 55 B4
Parkwood Rd BH21 55 C4
Pine Tree Clo BH21 55 D3
Poole Rd BH21 55 C4
Poplar Clo BH21 55 D3
Priors Walk BH21 55 B3
Pye Corner BH21 55 B3
Pye La BH21 55 B3
Quince La BH21 55 D2
Redcotts La BH21 55 B3
Redcotts Rd BH21 55 A3
Retreat Rd BH21 55 C4
Richmond Rd BH21 55 D4
River Clo BH21 55 C2
Riverside Pk BH21 55 D5
Rodway BH21 55 C4
Rowlands Hill BH21 55 C3
Royal Mews BH21 55 C3
Royston Dri BH21 55 C3
St Catherines BH21 55 C4
St Johns Clo BH21 55 C4
St Johns Hill BH21 55 C3
St Margarets
  Almshouses BH21 55 A3
St Margarets Clo BH21 55 A2
St Margarets Hill BH21 55 A2
School La BH21 55 B3
Shakespeare Rd BH21 55 B2
Sheppards Fld BH21 55 B2
Silverwood Clo BH21 55 D6
Sopwith Cres BH21 55 D6
Station Rd BH21 55 C5
Station Ter BH21 55 C4
Stevenson Clo BH21 55 C4
Stone La BH21 55 A2
Stone La Ind Est
  BH21 55 A2
Tapper Ct BH21 55 D4
Tennyson Rd BH21 55 B2
The Square BH21 55 B3
Three Lions Clo BH21 55 B3
Tower La BH21 55 D2
Trumpeters Ct BH21 55 B3
Ullswater Rd BH21 55 C5
Venator Pl BH21 55 C2
Victoria Pl BH21 55 A3
Victoria Rd BH21 55 A3
Walford Clo BH21 55 B1
Walford Gdns BH21 55 B2
Welland Rd BH21 55 C4
Wesley Rd BH21 55 D3
West Borough BH21 55 B2
West Row BH21 55 B3
West St BH21 55 B3
Westfield Clo BH21 55 D3
Whitehouse Rd BH21 55 C5
Whiteways BH21 55 D2
Willett Rd BH21 55 A5
Wimborne By-Pass
  BH21 55 A5
Wimborne Rd BH21 55 A4

Wimborne Rd BH21 55 B2
Wimborne Rd BH21 55 D2
Yew Tree Clo BH21 55 C3

WOOL

Baileys Dri BH20 56 B2
Baker Clo BH20 56 B2
Bindon La BH20 56 D2
Bindon Way BH20 56 D2
Breachfield BH20 56 C2
Burton Clo BH20 56 B2
Burton La BH20 56 A2
Burton Wood BH20 56 A2
Cedar Clo BH20 56 C2
Chalk Pit La BH20 56 B3
Church La BH20 56 D2
Colliers La BH20 56 C2
Cottage Clo BH20 56 C2
Dorchester Rd BH20 56 A3
Duck St BH20 56 D3
East Burton Rd BH20 56 A1
Fairfields BH20 56 D2
Folly La BH20 56 C2
Frome Av BH20 56 B2
Giddy Green La BH20 56 A2
Giddy Green Rd BH20 56 A2
High St BH20 56 D3
High Street Clo BH20 56 D2
Hillside Rd BH20 56 C3
Hyde Rd BH20 56 C2
Hyde Way BH20 56 D2
Jeremy Clo BH20 56 D2
Knowle Hill BH20 56 C2
Knowlewood Knap
  BH20 56 C3
Lampton Clo BH20 56 B2
Linclieth Rd BH20 56 C2
Locks Piece BH20 56 D2
Lower Hillside Rd
  BH20 56 C3
Lulworth Rd BH20 56 B3
Meadow La BH20 56 C2
Moreton Rd BH20 56 A2
New Buildings Rd
  BH20 56 A3
New Rd BH20 56 C3
Oakdene Rd BH20 56 B3
Quarr Hill BH20 56 D3
Sandhills Cres BH20 56 A2
Spring St BH20 56 D2
Swallows Clo BH20 56 C2
Station Rd BH20 56 C2
Sydenham Cres BH20 56 B2
The Alisons BH20 56 A2
The Cross BH20 56 D2
The Square BH20 56 C2
Vicarage Clo BH20 56 C3
Wareham Rd BH20 56 C1
Water Meadow La
  BH20 56 A1